To my parents, Rita and Jim, for their unceasing support without which this book – and my past 20 years exploring and experiencing Amish culture - would not have been possible. Everyone who enjoys this guide owes them a debt of gratitude. Thanks also to my wife, Rachel, for putting up with my Amish indulgences and accompanying me on many of my journeys.

THE WILLIAMS GUIDE TO AMISH COUNTRY

The inspiration for this book evolved over my two decades of exploring "Amish Country." But there was one moment in particular that began to shape this project. The night before my wedding, held near Zanesville, Ohio, I was in my hotel room watching The Weather Channel. Isn't that what every groom does the night before his wedding? In reality, I've always been a weather buff and our wedding was an outdoor event so I had good reason to be interested in what Mother Nature had in store the next day. There used to be a feature on The Weather Channel called "Local on the 8s" where they gave the local forecast at 8, 18, 28, 48, and 58 minutes after the hour. Based on where I was staying, the channel gave the forecast for Columbus, Zanesville, and "Amish Country." I couldn't help but chuckle. I was certain that the forecast was referring to the vast Amish community in eastern Ohio between Canton and Columbus. But, really, no single place lays claim to the title "Amish Country." Sure there are the typical locales like Lancaster, Pennsylvania, Holmes County, Ohio and Shipshewana, Indiana that grab the lion's share of the tourist traffic. But there are plenty of other places that can also rightfully stake their claim to being called "Amish Country."

"People from overseas want to visit three places when they come to the USA: the Grand Canyon, Disney World, and Amish Country," one business owner in Lancaster County's Amish tourism mecca told us. And plenty of people who live in the USA also flock to explore and enjoy Amish ambiance. Ohio's Amish country is the state's top tourism draw, ahead of the peaceful shores of Lake Erie and the wild rides of premiere parks like Cedar Point and Kings Island.

But for all the interest in visiting Amish country, there's never been a guide that puts it all together in one place. Until now. We hope you find this guide useful and interesting and that it will open your eyes to the vast array of opportunities for cultural exchange with the Amish. "Now, wait a second," you might say, "aren't the Amish a very private people? Wouldn't a book like this simply attract more tourists to a people who don't want them?" Fair premise, but inaccurate. More than fifty years ago the Amish generally lived in agrarian isolation. That's no longer the case. The majority of Amish now make their living in occupations other than farming: factory work, furniture-making, baking, cabinetry, and construction. Even the ones who do farm often have home-based businesses on the side such as selling eggs or local honey. Carefully choreographed tourism is essential to Amish culture. Commerce from tourism allows an Amish person to work from home and home and hearth are central to Amish life. An Amish person who is trying to earn a living selling furniture from a home-based shop welcomes customers. Tourism is the river that irrigates the valley of Amish economics. Tourism and the Amish share a symbiotic relationship: Amish entrepreneurs need the business, while outsiders need the solace and simplicity the rest of the world seems to sorely lack.

This book will show that whether you're seeking a slice of simplicity, the peaceful clip-clop of buggies, or some just-from-the-oven cinnamon rolls from an authentic Amish bakery, there are many places you can go. Smyrna, Maine; Pinecraft, Florida; Ethridge, Tennessee, these, and many more communities all can rightfully lay claim to the title "Amish Country." And this guide, for the first time, offers a comprehensive travel partner to plan your trip to Amish Country.

TIPS FOR MAKING THE MOST OF YOUR VISIT TO AMISH COUNTRY

We spend a lot of time in this book recommending visiting Amish-owned home-based businesses whether that be buying a dozen fresh eggs or stopping into a quilt shop. Visiting a home-based Amish business is a great way to make new friends and see their farmsteads first-hand. Always employ the "golden rule" when visiting an Amish home or business. Be respectful and courteous. You probably wouldn't want someone tromping through your flower beds or garden and peering in your windows, so it's a safe bet an Amish person doesn't want that either. Here are some other suggestions to make your trip more enjoyable:

Buy, don't browse. Time is money for most entrepreneurs and the Amish are no different. Don't visit a home-based Amish business and launch into a three-hour conversation about your grandchildren or garden back home. Do go in and exchange pleasantries and small talk, but even such small interactions should be accompanied by a purchase. Of course there are times when you're going to want to just browse and enjoy the craftsmanship at an Amish furniture store or quilt shop and that's great, just be respectful of the proprietor's time.

Cash, not Credit. The vast majority of Amish businesses do not accept credit cards. Some of the bigger bulk food stores and bakeries do, but they are still the exception rather than the rule. Most Amish businesses will accept checks but with horse and buggy being the main mode of transport, it can take a long time for a deposit to go through, so if you don't balance your checkbook methodically, a check hitting your account five months later can be a surprise. We once bought some cinnamon rolls from an Amish bake sale and the check was deposited three months later. So we like to use cash when shopping in Amish country, especially at the home-based businesses.

Photographic Politeness. There are a wide range of views within the Amish community about photography. Cameras are completely unwelcome in more conservative Amish settlements, while in a few they are accepted. In most, cameras are tolerated. Use the "Golden Rule", would YOU want someone sticking a camera in your face or treating you like a zoo animal? Probably not. This doesn't mean you can't get some amazing photos when visiting Amish country. The vast majority of Amish don't mind you photographing their buggies, colorful laundry on the lines, school-houses, windmills, and even their homes. Ask, whenever possible, even in these situations.

Be Flexible. Whenever possible we have added phone numbers to this book, but many Amish businesses don't have phones so calling ahead isn't always an option. Therefore don't be too let-down if you drive two hours to your favorite Amish store only to find that it is closed for the day because of a wedding in the community. Such things can and do occur, so have back-up plans in place. And do your homework before your trip so you can factor in local customs. For instance, in Kalona, Iowa (see page 87), most businesses are closed on Tuesdays. We haven't run into that in any other settlement. In northern Indiana, many Amish businesses are closed on Ascension Day, and that isn't something we've encountered in every community. Of course sometimes no matter how much homework you do, you could arrive at your favorite Amish business only to discover it is closed for the day because of a funeral or wedding. Weddings are often held on Thursdays, but we don't recommend not traveling to an Amish settlement on a Thursday on the off chance a wedding might be going on, but just to be flexible. If you are visiting

Amish Country you might want Sunday to be a "travel day" for you. Amish businesses are not open on Sunday.

Dress Modestly. We aren't saying to go on your Amish excursion in a moon-suit or burqa, but some decorum is often welcomed. In some Amish businesses we've actually seen signs saying "please dress modestly" or "modest attire appreciated." You'll generally be treated warmly in most Amish businesses whether you are wearing shorts and flip-flops or your church clothes, but many Amish appreciate the respect of covering yourself as much as possible. Again, if it's a sweltering summer day and you want to wear shorts because that's what is most comfortable, go ahead and do so, you won't be given the cold shoulder. But if all things are equal, opt for some khaki pants and a polo shirt for men, and women, a comfy dress..

Bike, Run, Walk, or Camp. While one of our favorite ways to explore Amish country is by just getting in the car and meandering back roads, we can't discount the value of immersing oneself in Amish culture beyond the confines of a car. Whether it be going for a run, a walk, or a bike ride, we try to include activities in this book that incorporate such alternative, active experiences.

Amish Pen Pals. One of the most frequent questions at The Williams Guide: "How do I go about finding an Amish pen pal?" Our first question, incredulously, is: "you mean people still write letters?" Just kidding. In this wired world there are still those who love to put pen to paper and express themselves the old-fashioned way. But at the risk of sounding like Mr. Rainy Parade, finding an Amish pen pal isn't easy. Outsiders are often fascinated and curious about the Amish, but that curiosity is seldom a two-way street. Keep in mind most Amish people see non-Amish (or English) every day in some capacity. Most of us don't see

Amish everyday unless you live near such a community (in which case you probably aren't clamoring for an Amish pen pal for the same reasons they are not seeking an English one). There's not much reciprocal curiosity, so I don't see lot of Amish people pining for a pen pal. So my advice: go about it how you would with someone non-Amish, make friends gradually and naturally and then write.

Church Services. Outsiders can and do join the Amish church. Successful conversions to the faith are rare, but not unheard of. This topic is a whole other book. But can a visitor who is interested in the faith attend an Amish church service? Well…that's tricky. The short answer is, yes: However, Old Order Amish services are held in private homes, not in a formal church building. So you'd sort of be crashing someone's private gathering if you just dropped in. The best way is to be invited. There are a few exceptions (see Unity, Maine, page 98)

Something to Keep In Mind. We refer to Amish settlements in this book by their postal address name. That's what most Amish people do, so that is what we'll do. But it can sometimes be a little confusing when trip planning. For instance, the "Rexford, Montana" Amish community is actually a 35 minute drive away from Rexford in an unincorporated area known as "West Kootenai." But since the area's postal address is Rexford, most Amish refer to their settlement by that name. So just because we call something the "Jamesport community" doesn't mean everything is right smack in that town. The Amish live in rural areas so plan for that.

AMISH CALENDAR

The Amish often observe special dates and holidays that most non-Amish do not. In our years visiting Amish Country we've been surprised on occasion to find one of our favorite Amish stores closed because of a wedding or an unanticipated holiday. Below is a calendar you might find helpful. Keep in mind that each Amish settlement is different and many have their own traditions and observances. What is observed one place may not be in another, so this is only meant as a guideline.

Old Christmas – January 7 (heavily observed in northern Indiana Amish settlements)

Easter Monday – Day after Easter Sunday

Ascension Day - Ascension Day is traditionally celebrated on a Thursday, the fortieth day of Easter (heavily observed in northern Indiana)

Pentecost Monday - Pentecost is celebrated 50 days (about seven weeks) after Easter Sunday, some Amish observe "Pentecost Monday", the day after Pentecost Sunday (heavily observed in Lancaster County).

October 11 – "Fall Fast Day" – This is an old holiday with deep religious roots, but it is only sporadically observed in Amish churches. This day is widely observed in Lancaster County, Pennsylvania's Amish community. When October 11 occurs on a Sunday, Amish will take the Saturday off to observe. So plan accordingly especially when planning a trip to Lancaster County or its daughter communities (for instance, Parke County or Wayne County, Indiana).

Other times and days of note: Although this is changing slowly, many Amish hold weddings on Thursdays. In northern settlements wedding season tends to run from June to September, while in more southern settlements it goes from November to March. Some Amish businesses may be closed if there is a wedding in the community.

Fast time vs. Slow Time - Some Amish communities don't observe daylight savings time. Geauga County, Ohio's Amish settlement and many Swartzentruber Amish churches do not observe the time change so plan accordingly.

USING THIS BOOK

This book is meant to make your travel to Amish country as enjoyable and worthwhile as possible. This is the first edition, we expect this guide will come out with revisions in the years ahead. We do not profess to include every single Amish or Mennonite settlement in this book. In future editions we would like to get to Daviess County, Indiana and Milverton, Ontario, for instance. If you find we missed a favorite Amish-owned business or there's a bed & breakfast in Amish country you'd like to recommend, kindly let us know if there's a favorite Amish B & B that we've missed by sending an email to **thewilliamsguide@gmail.com.** This book is not meant to be a scholarly interpretation of Amish life, although we do try to provide information and facts throughout. A really great guide to the Amish with a more scholarly/encyclopedic angle is *The Amish* by Don Kraybill, Steven Nolt, and Karen Johnson-Weiner.

We have grouped the book by geography so that you can quickly find the areas you wish to visit. For some Amish settlements that we've spent a lot of time visiting or that we felt there is plenty for visitors to do and experience, we have provided full community profiles with driving directions, lodging recommendations, and places to go to stock up on basics like camera batteries, memory cards, or picnic supplies.

Not every Amish settlement is the same. Some are extremely conservative, eschewing even indoor plumbing and orange safety triangles on their buggies, while others are more "progressive" with plumbing and telephones. We have described settlements using the following terminology:

SWARTZENTRUBER AMISH: This insular sect of the Amish is among the most conservative. Their buggies usually don't display the orange safety triangle and church members do not have telephones or indoor plumbing. Don't even think about taking your camera to a Swartzentruber church community.

OLD ORDER AMISH (conservative): While not Swartzentruber conservative, these settlements still hew very much to old ways. Cameras are generally not welcome and the communities may not be quite as receptive to outsiders. Sometimes they do not display the orange safety triangle on the back of their buggies. They speak German dialect as their first language at home.

OLD ORDER AMISH (traditional): Very classic Old Order Amish communities, a wide variation of views and of what technologies are acceptable and what aren't. They speak German dialect as their first language at home.

OLD ORDER AMISH (progressive): These communities tend to be more welcoming to outsiders, you may see cell phones in use and electricity in businesses. Photography is tolerated or in some cases accepted (again, common courtesy: ask anyone, Amish or non-Amish, before you take their photo). They speak German dialect as their first language at home, although a lot of English words are mixed in.

NEW ORDER AMISH: When people hear about this church they automatically assume it's more progressive, but that's not necessarily the case. This is a horse-and-buggy church that split from the Old Order Church over theological differences in the 1960s. New Order churches do tend to allow more technology like telephones and are generally more tolerant of photography. They are a more evangelical church than the Old Order. Another split formed the New New Order Amish or New Order Amish Fellowship. They speak German dialect as their first language at home, although a lot of English words are mixed in.

BEACHY AMISH MENNONITE: This can best be described as a "hybrid" church. They can actually be theologically more literal and evangelical than the Old Order Amish and they dress plainly and sometimes speak German at home, but they do allow cars and non-internet capable computers in their homes.

MENNONITE: The Mennonite church came first and the Amish split from them. The Mennonites have a very broad spectrum, from very progressive, non-plain to Old Order horse and buggy Mennonites.

BRETHREN: This is a Plain church that shares similarities with the Amish: pacifism, plain dress, and a separation from wider society, but they come from a more recent religious movement known as Pietism whereas the Amish and Mennonites come from the Anabaptist tradition.

PLAIN: We used the term "Plain" as a catch-all term for German Baptist, Amish, or Mennonites all whom use that word to describe themselves. The term is not derogatory, it refers to their style of dress, which is, indeed Plain. So when you see that word in the book, it's just a term used to describe one of the above groups.

CALIFORNIA

TUOLUMNE COUNTY

IMPORTANT AT-A-GLANCE INFORMATION

AFFILIATION: German Baptist

GETTING THERE: Take California 132 seven miles to Albers Road, continue onto South Yosemite Ave, and then turn right onto California 108 and follow 35 miles. Take the Mono Way exit toward Route 108.

The Golden State isn't the first place that comes to mind when one brings up Plain people. There are, however, a handful of Plain settlements in California. As of 2013 there are no Amish communities in the state, but there is a small Mennonite settlement near Lebec about an hour north of Los Angeles, and a community of German Baptists near Bangor in the far north. But the largest Plain presence are the German Baptists around Modesto.

For those who want to experience a slice of "California Plain", a stop to Cover's Apple Ranch is a must. The 89-acre ranch is one of the few remaining orchards in an area that used to boast dozens. Cover's is perched at 3000 feet in the foothills of the Sierra Nevada Mountains, 19211 Cherokee Road, Tuolumne, CA 95379, phone 209-928-4689, a cool, crisp climate ideal for an orchard. Cover's claim to fame with customers is their "Mile High Pie".

The Mile High Pie is a sinful confection packed with 10 cups of apples.

Another aspect of Cover's that we love is their every Friday night reservations-only supper. Dinner and dessert are all included for one price. The supper is a rare opportunity to experience the deep traditions of Brethren baking and cooking. The Cover family are members of the Brethren church and dress plainly, so are often mistaken for Amish.

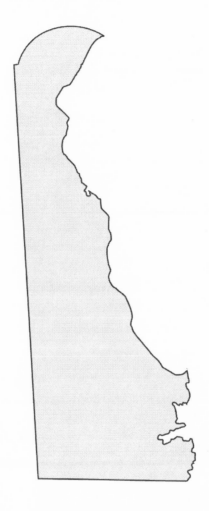

DELAWARE

Delaware's Amish presence is over a century old, but such a small state doesn't have a sprawling population.

DOVER

IMPORTANT AT-A-GLANCE INFORMATION

AFFILIATION: Old Order Amish, traditional

LODGING: There are plenty of chain motels in Dover proper.

PROVISIONS: We like Safeway, 190 John Hunn Brown Road, Dover, DE 19901, phone 302-730-9100, which offers a full line of groceries and picnic provisions.

FOOD: No Amish restaurants, but plenty of dining choices in Dover. We recommend packing a picnic and eating your lunch in Amish Country.

GETTING THERE: From Baltimore, Washington or Richmond via the Chesapeake Bay Bridge, take US 50/301 across the bridge. Follow US 301 North to Maryland Route 302 (right turn at mile marker 102). Turn right on Maryland Route 454 at Templeville. Route 454 becomes Route 8 at the Delaware state line, take to Dover.

From South of the Chesapeake Bay via Chesapeake Bay Bridge:

Take I-64 West to Richmond, then I-95 North to the Washington Beltway (I-495 North). Take I-495 North to Route 50/301. Take Route 50/301 East over the Chesapeake Bay Bridge. Follow US 301 North to Maryland Route 302 (right turn at mile marker 102). Turn right Maryland Route 454 at Templeville. Route 454 becomes Route 8 at the Delaware state line to Dover.

From Areas Served by the Pennsylvania Turnpike:

Take the turnpike east to the Valley Forge Exit, then US 202 South. Take I-95 South to I-495 South via Exit 11 towards Port of Wilmington/ Baltimore. I-495S becomes I-95S. Merge onto DE 1 South via exit 4A towards Christiana/Mall Road (Portions toll). Follow Route 1 South to Exit 104 (50 cent toll/exact change only at night). Turn left on US 13 South.

BRIEFLY

The Old Order Amish community in Delaware is the closest to the ocean, which means Amish families frequently take picnics to the beach and get to enjoy the water.

HISTORY AND INDEPTH

"Delaware is the only state in the country that just allows the Amish to settle in three counties," an Amish woman who lives here told us.

"What?" we gasped at hearing such a thing. We had never heard of such restrictive laws elsewhere and it seemed downright illegal to regulate by religion.

"Of course, Delaware only has three counties!" the Amish woman deadpanned.

As one of the smallest states, the Amish here have one of the most welcoming attitudes. Whether it be in their wit or the annual bike tour, visitors won't leave this community feeling unloved. There are nine church districts in this Amish community, which was founded in 1915.

There are a couple of "signature events" to keep on your calendar when visiting the Amish community here.

AMISH COUNTRY BIKE TOUR

We love this event because it is so accessible and the Amish community is really involved. First, accessible. Yes, there are 50, 62, and even 100 mile loops through the bucolic Delaware countryside for hard-core cyclists, but there are also 15 and 25 mile loops over landscape that is forgiving and flat. The courses are sprinkled with plenty of comfort stations. The comfort station is at the Amish school-house where members of the community serve homemade pies and cookies. Part of the proceeds from the bike tour go to benefit the Amish school, while the rest is divided among other local organizations. This is, by the way, a bike tour, not a bike race. You will see families with children biking alongside more seasoned cyclists. A local Amish man leads the pack of cyclists with his horse-drawn buggy to start the tour. Another local Amish entrepreneur sells a sweet ending to the event by offering up homemade ice cream made with some large contraption that some people say reminds them of the game Mouse Trap. For more information or to register, visit amishcountrybiketour.com. The Amish Country Bike Tour is held the second Saturday of September.

AMISH AUCTION

The third Saturday of each October features the annual school auction to benefit the Amish parochial school. The auction launched in 1991 and has been going strong ever since.

"It's a great opportunity for quilt collectors and enthusiasts to review and bid on hundreds of styles of quilts," Robin Coventry, Director of Public Relations and Special Events for Kent County Tourism told the *Sussex Countian* newspaper. "There are so many quilts it is almost overwhelming."

In addition to quilts, there are crafts, baked goods, and furniture for sale. We love the timing of this auction on the cusp of crisp autumn days in the Delaware countryside. The auction is held at the Ammon Miller Farm at 3312 Yoder Drive, Dover, DE.

The Dover Amish community is located west of the city and Yoder Drive is in the heart of it, a great place to car cruise and savor some of the serene scenes of well-kept Amish farmsteads, colorful laundry airing on the lines, and home-based businesses offering anything from fresh eggs to honor-system tomatoes.

Other Amish businesses we like:

BYLER'S COUNTRY STORE, 1368 Rose Valley School Road, Dover, DE 19904, phone 302-674-1631. This is a classic Amish country store featuring wood stoves, groceries, bakery section and bulk foods.

DANIEL YODER'S FURNITURE SHOP, 462 Rose Valley School Road, Dover, DE 19904, this is a wonderful outlet for hand-made Amish craftsmanship made and sold onsite, an increasing rarity with Amish furniture.

FLORIDA

The Sunshine State isn't typically associated with the Amish. In fact, there is only one Amish settlement in the entire state. It's a place called Pinecraft tucked away in a quiet corner of Sarasota.

SARASOTA

FOOD: Several Sarasota restaurants offer traditional Amish fare and are the highlight of any visit to Pinecraft (see below).

GETTING THERE: From Tampa take I-75 South towards Naples. Drive 45 miles to exit 210 toward Sarasota/St. Armands. Merge into Fruitville Road. Turn left onto South Beneva Road. Turn right onto Bahia Vista.

From Naples, take I-75 north 103 miles. Take exit 207 towards Florida 758 West. Turn left onto Bee Ridge Road. Turn right onto Cattlemen Road and left onto Bahia Vista. Follow Bahia Vista 5 miles into the Pinecraft community.

OTHER ATTRACTIONS: We recommend Myakka River State Park, 13208 State Road 72, Sarasota, FL 34241, phone 941-361-6511, as a fun side trip. And Lido Key accessible by drawbridge from downtown Sarasota offers hours of unique boutiques, eclectic and elegant restaurants, and mouth-watering flavors of ice cream.

IMPORTANT AT-A-GLANCE INFORMATION

AFFILIATION: Beachy Amish Mennonite off-peak; Plain people of all groups during peak season.

LODGING: Plenty of chain motels in the area. See Editor's Choice.

PROVISIONS: Sweet Bay Foods and Publix are two popular chain groceries that are ubiquitous in the area. A Super Target at 101 N Cattlemen Road, Sarasota, FL 34243, phone 941-360-7520, provides an everything-under-one-roof shopping experience.

OTHER: Bring your swim-suit and snorkels, the nearby Siesta Key Beach is consistently rated one of the best in the USA for its warm waters, white sand, and gorgeous sunsets.

EDITOR'S CHOICE: Stay at The Ringling Beach House, 523 Beach Road, Sarasota, FL 34242, phone 941-349-1236, only a 10 minute drive from the Amish settlement. Plenty of Amish frequent Siesta Key's beaches. As the name implies these quaint quarters used to be the winter home of the Ringling Brothers circus. There are 10 units with names like The Flying Trapeze, the Lion, The Elephant, and the Ringmaster. Each one is more like a mini-apartment with a sitting area and fully functional kitchen. Yoder's Restaurant, 3434 Bahia Vista Street, Sarasota, FL 34239, phone 941-955-7771, is our top Pinecraft pick for a meal.

BRIEFLY

Pinecraft is the only Amish community in Florida and the only one where sunscreen and swim-suits are more common than buggies. In fact, you won't see any buggies here.

HISTORY AND INDEPTH INFORMATION

You could easily plan a wonderful family beach vacation in nearby Siesta Key and add a splash of Amish to it by visiting the nearby enclave of Pinecraft. Or if you only have a little time, you can enjoy a meal in this neighborhood and experience some unique Amish ambiance. The Amish first ventured to this quiet corner of Sarasota in the 1920s, lured to the area by the promise of lucrative celery farming. The celery farms turned out to be a land scam, but the Amish who came liked what they saw, finding the climate curative and the nearby beach to be relaxing. Ever since those first arrivals discovered the pleasantry of Pinecraft there has been a growing Plain presence here. Amish and Mennonites of varying levels of scriptural strictness come to Pinecraft to figuratively and sometimes literally let their hair down.

The Pinecraft of today is quite different than the one that the Amish happened upon in the 1920s. The climate is still therapeutic and the warm waters of the Gulf just as inviting, but sprawling Sarasota has enveloped Pinecraft on all sides. Still, despite being surrounded by city, Pinecraft retains a type of small-town charm.

We think Pinecraft almost has a "college town" feel in the sense that it's packed during one half of the year, and the other half the year is left to the locals. The peak time for Pinecraft is from November through March. That is when the snowbirds descend on this tiny enclave for a stint under the West Florida sun. Shuffleboard courts are packed, it's tough to find a table at area restaurants, and the streets are filled with Plain people of all persuasions. One Amish boy asked with wide-eyed wonder upon arrival: "Where do they keep their horses?" The answer: they don't. The mode of transport of choice in Pinecraft are "Florida Buggies", otherwise known as adult tricycles. Most Amish and Mennonite visitors pedal these ubiquitous trikes on their village errands to and from the post office, Yoder's or the park. For longer trips, perhaps to the nearby Siesta Key Beach, the Sarasota city bus system is popular.

On Mondays, Wednesdays, and Fridays at 12:30 p.m. during peak season the Pioneer Bus rumbles into town from the north. This Ohio-based bus line devotes most of its business to connecting Amish customers in Ohio and Indiana with the enclave of Pinecraft. The passengers disembark, squinting in the bright noon sun, with a mixture of weariness after a 20 hour drive and excitement at arriving in this Amish paradise. Crowds sometimes gather to watch the arriving snowbirds greeting them with a welcome as warm as the Florida sun.

You'll want to check out one of several Amish-themed restaurants that keep people satiated here. First and foremost, we recommend **Yoder's Restaurant** at 3434 Bahia Vista Street, Sarasota, FL 34239, phone 941-955-7771. Their ample, moist fried chicken with its crispy skin has been featured on the Food Network's Man vs. Food and their pies attract a passionate following. The peanut butter pie is legendary. In fact, we once were driving from Naples to catch a flight out of Tampa. We figured we had enough time for a quick detour into Pinecraft to buy a slice of Yoder's peanut butter pie to savor on the way to the airport. Not factoring in Tampa traffic we almost missed our flight. You know what? For a chance to taste a piece of Yoder's mouth-melting peanut butter pie, missing a flight almost would have been worth it!

Yoder's Restaurant opened its doors in 1975 and has served as the centerpiece of Pinecraft ever since. Amanda Yoder became legendary for her pies. Not surprisingly Thanksgiving is the "pie peak" as holiday meals all around west Florida get rounded out by Yoder's pumpkin, pecan and peanut butter pies. And if you happen to be there in the fall, don't forget to try the pumpkin pancakes, a seasonal specialty offering a whiff and hint of spices slathered in maple syrup. A gift shop at Yoder's offers an array of crafts and even the Amish newspaper, The Budget, for sale.

If you are limited on time and you can only choose one restaurant in Pinecraft, we recommend Yoder's. But if you're going to be lingering in Pinecraft for a while, why not eat your way through the village? You can't really go wrong with any of the restaurants. While none rises to the level of Yoder's, in our opinion, here are some other ones worth checking out:

TROYER'S DUTCH HERITAGE (formerly Der Dutchman) - is a sprawling complex across busy Bahia Vista Road from Yoder's. It is the largest Amish restaurant and gift shop in the Sarasota area and is owned by Ohio-based Dutch Hospitality Group which operates several large restaurants in various Amish communities. Troyer's offers a hot buffet filled with traditional favorites and a salad bar offering up traditional Pennsylvania Dutch fare. Address and hours: 3713 Bahia Vista Street, Sarasota, FL 34232, phone 941-955-8007, Days/Hours of Operation: Monday through Thursday, 6 AM to 8 PM; Friday and Saturday, 6 AM to 9 PM; Closed Sunday

Meals Served: Breakfast 6 AM to 11 AM; Lunch 11 AM to 4 PM; Dinner 4 PM until Close.

MILLER'S DUTCH KITCHEN – We place a premium on Amish-inspired restaurants that really "get it right" and Miller's does. That's because the owners are of Amish heritage and this is reflected in their menu. The restaurant is located in neighboring Bradenton about 20 minutes north of Pinecraft but well worth the drive if you are doing the "Amish restaurant circuit." Or if you are on your way back north, Miller's is a great stopping point for a final meal before you hit the road. The ornate two-story building houses the restaurant on the first floor and the newly-renovated gift shop on the second floor. Miller's Dutch Kitchen also serves a breakfast buffet from 7 AM to 11 AM Monday through Saturday. Address: 3401 14th St W, Bradenton, FL 34205, phone 941-746-8253, Days/Hours of Operation: Monday through Saturday, 7 AM to 8 PM; Closed Sunday, Meals Served: Breakfast, Lunch, Dinner.

Ah, and dessert! While you are eating your way through Pinecraft if you are tired of pie (really, though, does anyone ever get tired of pie?), the next best thing might be some ice cream and there's no more revered institution in Pinecraft than Big Olaf's Creamery.

BIG OLAF'S CREAMERY: This Mennonite-owned local ice cream chain describes their ice cream as "every tub of Big Olaf Ice Cream is hand mixed with the finest ingredients and is then churned in batch freezers by local Amish Craftsmen." Offering flavors from butter pecan to amaretto almond, Big Olaf's is a favorite stop for Plain people and English alike. There are two locations, one in the heart of Pinecraft at 3350 Bahia Vista Street, Sarasota, FL 34239, phone 941-726-3800, and if you prefer to enjoy your ice cream on soft sand and in front of lapping waves there is a location on Siesta Key.

When you snap out of your food coma there are other places to visit in and around Pinecraft to enjoy Amish culture.

ALMA SUE'S QUILTS, 3737 Bahia Vista St Sarasota, FL (941) 330-0993: We are very enthusiastic about this store because it's one of the few places we know of where you can just walk into a public business and see the actual Amish-Mennonite craft of quilting occurring.

You can watch the quilting, ask questions of the Amish and Mennonite quilters, and enjoy the special ambiance of Pinecraft. During the busy season (January – March) there are usually three quilts in frame with 15 to 16 Amish and/or Mennonite women all sitting around hand-quilting during the work day. They are paid per yard and the different craftswomen get to work, each focusing on their specialty.

"Some ladies like to sew tops, some don't do tops but they like to stitch," explains store owner Ella Miller Toy, explaining that while you can go into the store and buy quilts off the rack, custom quilting is the store's biggest business. Even during the slow summer season some of the year-round Pinecraft Amish or Mennonite residents come in to quilt. Toy herself is Mennonite and was raised near Ohio's largest Amish and Mennonite settlement.

Miller's Dutch Haus Furniture, 3737 Bahia Vista Street, Sarasota, FL 34232, phone 941-952-5646, offers an authentic array of Amish-inspired and hand-crafted furniture of all types. It's right next to Troyer's Dutch Heritage, so waddle on over after a big meal.

One of our favorite Pinecraft pastimes is to visit "the park." **Pinecraft Park,** as it is formally known, is a wonderful place to just sit and people watch or enjoy that Big Olaf's cone. During peak season the park belongs to the Plain people. Shuffleboard courts become packed places of good-natured ribbing and friendly competition. One lane is always reserved for the ladies, where bonnet-clad, plainly dressed women can be seen engaged in white-knuckle games, Suspender-clad, bearded men crowd the rest of the courts. Alligators lull in the lagoon nearby seemingly oblivious to the nearby swarm of people.

No visit to Pinecraft would be complete without a short road trip to **Myakka Lake State Park,** 13208 State Road 72, Sarasota, FL 34241, phone 941-361-6511. This is one of Florida's oldest and largest state parks and an important preservation part of the upper Everglades basin. The park features a unique "canopy walk" and tower that takes visitors up into the tree tops and high above them for a breath-taking panorama of the surrounding countryside. Airboat rides and a snack bar that offers "alligator nuggets" are all part of the experience. Many Amish and Plain people include this as part of their Florida experience during the peak season. We often have enjoyed the company of Amish and Mennonites who are visiting the park when we are.

The busy season culminates in the annual Pinecraft Days Arts and Craft Festival held each March at the Beneva Marketplace, 1235 Beneva Road, Sarasota, FL 34232. Call the Marketplace at 941-366-1234 to find out the time and date this year.

One of the things we recommend is simply cruising the small lanes and alleys of Pinecraft admiring the well-kept often thimble-sized winter refuges of the Amish. On Sunday mornings you might see a yard packed with bicycles (instead of buggies). This is the Pinecraft Amish church. Since the Amish typically hold worship services in private homes (as opposed to churches) the Pinecraft community presented a dilemma of sorts. Most homes are too small for a typical church service to be held so several years ago funds were pooled to buy one of the few large homes in Pinecraft. It was "hollowed out" into an open floor plan and that is where the more conservative Amish attend services during the winter.

During the peak snowbird season you'll make all sort of discoveries among the cottages and shotgun homes: yard sales, Amish auctions, and the occasional bake sale.

So, pack your swim-trunks and prepare to enjoy a great vacation, with one foot in Amish country, the other foot in the soft sand of Siesta!

GEORGIA

MONTEZUMA, GEORGIA

Amish and Mennonite settlements are few and far between in the Deep South of the United States. Historically their roots have been Midwestern and eastern, but slowly more buggies can be heard clattering down roads south of the Mason-Dixon Line. Montezuma, Georgia offers a wonderful Plain experience in the heart of the state's peach and peanut country. While this is not a horse and buggy community, it is a Beachy Amish Mennonite settlement. Church members dress plainly and are often mistaken for their more conservative cousins in the Amish faith, but the Beachy Amish allow automobiles and electricity. Still, Montezuma offers a wonderful opportunity to experience Amish-Mennonite culture in an area where such occasions are rare.

IMPORTANT AT-A-GLANCE INFORMATION

AFFILIATION: Beachy Amish Mennonite

GETTING THERE: Take exit 127 off of I-75 and head west about 10 miles on Georgia 26. Here are some places you'll want to visit:

YODER'S COUNTRY MARKET, 7401 Georgia 26: This is a classic Amish-Mennonite bulk food store, offerings all sorts of spices, prepackaged snacks, and a deli on-site.

Yoder's Deitsch Haus Restaurant and Bakery, 5252 State Route 26Phone: 478-472-2024: We love recommending this unassuming restaurant because it is such a rarity to eat in an actual Plain-owned and operated eatery. This southern gem fits the bill. And here you get a fusion of Amish meets Southern. Amish classics like fried chicken and carrot casserole mingle on the menu with southern specialties like cornbread and hummingbird cake. Adding to the dining bliss: this is a cafeteria, an old-fashioned serve-your-self cafeteria, so you can sample whatever you like! The restaurant's hours are a little hopscotch, it is closed Sunday and Monday and on Wednesday it is lunch only. Thursday through Saturday it is open for supper. Hours are as follows:

Lunch 11:30 - 2:00

Dinner 5:00 - 8:30

WHITE HOUSE FARM BED & BREAKFAST, 1679 Mennonite Church Road, phone 478-472-7942: Again, this is a rarity: a chance to actually stay at a Plain-owned bed & breakfast. This country delight is run by the Nisly family, one of the original settlers of the Mennonite settlement. Guests can stay in one of several rooms in this farmstead run by Larry and Amy Nisly. A full breakfast prepared in the Mennonite tradition of scratch baking is included in your stay.

KAUFFMAN'S FARM MARKET, Kauffman's Farmarket 1305 Mennonite Church Road Montezuma, Ga 31063 478-472-8833: An organic u-pick strawberry farm that offers up such specialties as homemade strawberry lemonade in season. Peaches, figs, and other southern favorites are grown at this Plain-owned market.

ILLINOIS

For much of the past century there was really only one place in Illinois with a sizable Amish presence: the Arthur-Arcola area. And while Arthur remains the largest community in the state, Amish settlements have sprung up throughout the Land of Lincoln over the past decade or so. There's a small Amish settlement near Flat Rock, Illinois and a larger one near Carrier Mills. Both of these are in the south, but Amish communities have also been established in the western part of the state also, in Pike County.

ILLINOIS

ARTHUR

ARTHUR

GETTING THERE: East access from I-57, take Exit 203 Illinois Route 133 west into Arthur.

OTHER ATTRACTIONS: For old-time interstate highway tourist kitsch, check out Rockome Gardens, 125 N. County Road 425E, Arcola, IL 61910, phone 217-268-4106. Rockome is a combination cheese factory, restaurant, and Amish emporium.

IMPORTANT AT-A-GLANCE INFORMATION

AFFILIATION: Traditional Amish, Plain Mennonite.

LODGING: Plenty of chain motels in the Mattoon-Charleston area or Decatur.

PROVISIONS: An old-fashioned IGA Foodliner, 215 South Vine Street, Arthur, IL 61911, phone 217-543-2633, serves the area from Arthur offering a full line of deli foods and picnic supplies.

FOOD: Yoder's Kitchen, 1195 East Columbia Street, Arthur, IL 61911, phone 217-543-2714. Roselen's, 1045 East Columbia Street, Arthur, IL 61911, phone 217-543-3106. Doris Yoder's Home meals (see below for info).

BRIEFLY

The Amish community around Arthur is by far the oldest and largest settlement in the Land of Lincoln. Only in the past 20 years have Amish churches begun to crop up in other parts of the state.

HISTORY AND INDEPTH

This is a settlement that we really like. What it lacks in scenic beauty, it makes up for in sheer size and depth of Amish ambiance. This Amish community was one of the pioneers in developing a "sustainable shop culture." What do we mean by that? Over 20 years ago the local tourism bureau created a map of Amish-owned businesses in the area that visitors could follow for a day-long driving tour. Fast forward to today and one Amish leader in the community estimates there are 900 (no, that isn't a typo, we'll say it again, nine hundred) Amish-owned generally home-based businesses.   With that many Amish-owned businesses to explore, you can keep yourself busy here for days on end.

This Amish settlement is tough to pin down ideologically. In some ways it's quite progressive. It's home to the only Amish-owned coffee-shop and drive-thru anywhere that we know of. Yet it also has a conservative streak such as when Amish made their displeasure known with a bike trail that was being built in their area. The thought of Lycra clad cyclists pedaling their way through such a conservative area had some upset.

One thing that won't happen if you visit Arthur: you won't leave hungry. For its size the Arthur community offers several authentically Amish dining options.

YODER'S KITCHEN: You can't beat Yoder's Kitchen for convenience and portions. Heaping helpings of Amish-style entrees like fried chicken, noodles, stuffing and plenty of pie for dessert. 1195 E Columbia, Arthur, IL 61911 Telephone: 217-543-2714. Regular Hours Mon - Sat: 7am - 8pm, Lunch Buffet Mon - Sat: 10:30am - 4pm Dinner Buffet Mon - Sat: 4:30pm - 8pm, Breakfast Buffet Fri (May – Dec) Sat (Year Round): 7am - 10:30am.

THE KITCHEN OF DORIS YODER: We have not sampled this place so we can't vouch for it. However, the opportunity to dine in an Amish home. Doris Yoder, an Old Order Amish woman, opens up her home for group meals by reservation. Meals are family-style, all you can eat. Phone 217-543-3409 to make a reservation. We've heard varying reviews about this place, please email us at **thewilliamsguide@gmail. com** with any comments about your experience here and we'll update this in future editions.

WHAT IS AMISH COOKING?

What IS Amish cooking anyway? Seven sweets and seven sours? No, that is more commonly associated with the food lore of Pennsylvania Dutch cooking, which is very different (but often confused with) Amish cooking. We wrote extensively about *Amish Cooks Across America* (Andrews McMeel Universal, 2012), available from your favorite bookseller. We can best define Amish cooking as back-to-basics country cooking. Historically, Amish homemakers had to make do with very little. They lived traditionally agrarian lives and during lean years an Amish cook might have to be especially creative about stretching ingredients to feed a large family. So when you think of Amish cooking it means nothing fancy, homemade noodles, bread stuffings, scratch-made bread, pan fried chicken, home-butchered meats, thick gravies, and lots of pie. In recommending Amish restaurants we look for ones that fulfill these very basic parameters but do so in an authentic way.

ROSENLEN'S COFFEE & DELIGHTS: This is one of our favorite places to recommend in Arthur. Roselen's is a coffee-shop (complete with a drive-through) owned and operated by two Amish sisters. Some people jokingly refer to it as "The Amish Starbucks." In addition to Starbucks-like beverage specialties, Roselen's offers a selection of sandwiches and pastries. Homemade bologna, scratch-made ice cream cakes, and other pastries are on the menu. Seeing horse-drawn buggies using the convenient drive-thru window isn't uncommon. Roselen's is located at 1045 East Columbia Street, Arthur, IL 61911, phone 217-543-3106.

After filling your belly at one of the above establishments, make sure you have plenty of cash on hand and start heading for the rural roads outside of Arthur. Start your day at Beachy's Bulk Foods. This is a very typical Amish-owned bulk food store (which is a good thing; we like typical Amish-owned bulk food stores). Shoppers rave about their selection of bulk grains, flours, spices, and spelt. Plenty of baking supplies and flours of all kinds. If you are lucky enough to be at Beachy's on a Friday or Saturday you'll be greeted with a selection of homemade pies and pastries for sale. Beachy's Bulk Foods is located at 259 N CR 200E, Arthur, IL 61911, phone 217-543-3447.

The Arthur Amish Country Cheese Festival held every Labor Day weekend is one of the area's signature events that bring Amish and English together. One of the festivals drawing cards: free cheese samples galore! This area has a rich cheese-making history, although most of that industry has moved on.

INDIANA

Indiana's Plain population is large and diverse. In Hoosierland you can find settlements of Amish, Mennonite, and Brethren. In the north, you have the sprawling third largest Amish settlement in the world. Around Berne and Grabill you'll find the unique Swiss Amish. Wayne and Parke Counties are home to "Lancaster County" Amish named after their Pennsylvania roots. And throughout the southern part of the state you'll find small Amish communities dotted, from ultra-conservative Swartzentruber settlements to the mixed Swiss-traditional community near Milroy. There's even a community of horse and buggy German Baptists near Flora. For its sheer diversity, Indiana is one of our favorite places to explore and experience Plain culture..

BERNE-GENEVA

IMPORTANT AT-A-GLANCE INFORMATION

AFFILIATION: Swiss Amish

LODGING: There are chain motels in nearby Decatur and Portland. The Clock Tower Inn, 1335 US Highway 27N, Berne, IN 46711, phone 260-589-8955, provides close accommodations to the center of the Amish settlement.

PROVISIONS: There is a Community Market in Berne that offers a full of line of groceries and supplies.

FOOD: No Amish restaurants in the area, but the White Cottage in downtown Berne sells a local specialty: pork tenderloin sandwich. These are a hit in Hoosierland, a huge piece of pork spilling over the ends of the bun breaded and fried. White Cottage is located at 178 West Main Street, Berne, IN 46711, phone 260-589-1432.

GETTING THERE: From Fort Wayne, take US 27 South 30 miles to Berne. From Indianapolis, stay on I-69 N for 73 miles. Exit I-69 at the Warren/Berne exit (exit 73) toward Warren. You'll follow a curving road into Warren. As you come into Warren turn right (west) at the first intersection onto State Road 218. Continue on SR 218 for 29.6 miles until you reach Berne. (You'll cross State Road 3 and Highway 1 before arriving in Berne.)

OTHER ATTRACTIONS: The Berne area is rather remote, but the city of Fort Wayne is only an hour away with shopping malls, a well-regarded zoo, and plenty of parks. The cities of Dayton, Indianapolis and Toledo are also only several hours away.

EDITOR'S CHOICE: We recommend staying at the Clock Tower Inn, 1335 US Highway 27N, Berne, IN 46711, phone 260-589-8955, for easy access to all of the area's Amish amenities.

BRIEFLY

This is one of the most unusual Amish communities in the country because of the Swiss heritage of this group. This is not a settlement that has a ton of tourist amenities but is definitely worth a day trip if you are seeking something a little different.

HISTORY AND IN DEPTH INFORMATION

One of the first things an outsider notices about the buggies in the Berne and Geneva area is the lack of a roof. A local Amish man chuckled and said "we like to call our buggies topless." Many of the reasons behind the origins of the settlement's unique traditions have been lost to time. But one of the best explanations we've been given for why the buggies have no roofs dates back the Victorian era. Covered carriages were a sign of an ornate aristocracy, the trappings of which this conservative Amish settlement rejected. So even today long after cars have replaced carriages in most of the world, the Amish here maintain the open buggies. It is not uncommon to see a family huddled together under thick blankets riding in an open buggy on an icy winter day. Or during the harsh heat of summer families will often savor the shade of a large black umbrella on their buggy to shield them from the sometimes unforgiving Indiana July sun.

One of our favorite things to do when visiting this community is to just get in the car and cruise. The majority of the area's Amish live to the east of Berne and Geneva and hours can enjoyably be spent driving and exploring the grid of roads. You'll be rewarded with scenes of crisp, colorful laundry in the unique Berne blues drying on lines (Monday is a popular wash day), you'll see quaint hand-lettered signs offering anything and everything from local honey to fresh eggs for sale from Amish homes, and if you're lucky you'll find baked goods being sold (usually on Fridays and Saturdays). If it's a Thursday during the spring, summer or autumn you might stumble upon a wedding gathering punctuated by a sea of open buggies parked in a field. We can't emphasize enough to be respectful of such gatherings. We think the vast majority of Amish attendees don't mind someone discreetly taking a photo of a field full of buggies, but trying to snap a shot of the bride and groom or in any way crashing the wedding is rude and disrespectful. Let your eyes be your camera.

The signature event of the year in Berne occurs on the final Friday and Saturday of July when the town holds its annual Swiss Days Festival. Here the Amish and English come together and celebrate the area's insular and unique Swiss heritage. This is a two-day showcase of all things Swiss and the unique Indiana-Swiss mish-mash that this area has become. The festival offers yodeling demonstrations, cheese-making workshops, and a pancake and sausage breakfast.

Be sure to visit the The Muensterberg Plaza and Clock Tower, North Church Avenue, in downtown Berne, an awe-inspiring and graciously soaring tribute to the monument of similar stature in its namesake European counterpart. Watch the glockenspiel presentation live each day at the clock tower plaza at noon, 3, 6, and 9 p.m. and wander the gorgeous "quilt garden" at the tower's base, a riot of colorful flowers patterned after the area's rich Amish quilt heritage.

The First Mennonite Church, 566 West Main Street, Berne, IN 46711, phone 260-589-3108, is symbolic of the area's Swiss heritage. The congregation boasts that the church has the largest sanctuary of any church in the USA.

There are a couple of noteworthy museums in the area that incorporate the Amish into the area's history and heritage. No visit to the Berne settlement is complete without stopping in at the Swiss Heritage Village, 1200 Swissway Road, Berne, IN 46711, phone 260-589-8007, the largest outdoor museum in northern Indiana. The village is a period recreation of Mennonite frontier life in the mid and late 1800s. Guided tours of the grounds are offered from 10 a.m. to 4 p.m. each day. Highlights include a cider press, cheese house, doctor's office, and sawmill all restored pristinely to their original state. Visiting the area's Amish is in many ways a step back into life a century ago. Step back a half century yet again by visiting this museum.

Geneva is a sleepy town a couple of miles south of Berne along US-27. The Limberlost State Historic Site, 200 East 6th Street, Geneva, IN 46740, phone 260-368-7428, preserves the works and life of the town's most famous resident: writer Gene Stratton Porter. She was the Barbara Kingsolver of her day, selling millions of copies of her works which often featured the local Limberlost swamp as a setting. Very little remains of what was once a vast swamp at the headwaters of the Wabash River. Pop into the Highline Restaurant, 404 E Line Street, Geneva, IN 46740, phone 260-368-7623, for classic Mom & Pop diner fare and then continue to explore the Amish settlement.

Also outside of Geneva is Amishville USA, 844 E 900 South, Geneva, IN 46740, phone 260-589-8780. Despite the kitschy name this is actually a pleasant, peaceful campground right in the heart of the area's Amish country. The campground accommodates anything from the most high-end RVs to primitive tent camping on its 120 acre grounds. The Amishville USA restaurant is open to campers and visitors alike and offers traditional Indiana fare.

Pssst!

Here's a something not widely known about the Berne settlement: this is one of the only Amish communities in the country where yodeling is commonly practiced. Since the Amish here are direct descendants of Swiss immigrants to the New World they retain many traditions and customs not found in other communities. Yodeling is one of them. This isn't the classic yodel-he-hee-ho popularized on TV, this is an exotic enchanting music. The Amish generally do not employ instruments, so use of voice in making music is all they have. The yodeling kicks it up a notch. The musical tradition gets passed down from generation to generation with sometimes several generations sitting around a supper table yodeling. The average visitor to Berne probably won't get to hear much yodeling, but we do have a free audio clip on our website of classic Swiss style yodeling at: **thewilliamsguide.com/ yodel**

Other "did you knows?" about the Berne-Geneva community:

The dialect spoken among the Amish here is a type of Bernese Swiss that is quite different from the variation of German. In fact, the dialect spoken here is so different that Amish from here have difficulty understanding the more common Germanic dialect spoken in other communities.

There are several "daughter" communities of Berne where the same language and customs persist, the largest is Seymour, Missouri

There are other differences that accentuate the Berne Amish from others, from culinary quirks to customs. For instance, raisin pie is a common confection served at weddings and celery is usually found on wedding tables in vases as both a décor and symbol – some say – of fertility. The celery is not often found in other Amish areas. Raisin pie is a funeral culinary tradition in other Amish communities elsewhere.

HIGHWAY HOP: RICHMOND, IN

We can't justify a separate entry in this book for one of Indiana's newest Amish communities, but if you're passing by on I-70 it is absolutely worth a stop. Because of its proximity to Interstate 70, one of the most heavily traveled east-west arteries in the USA, we christen this Amish community "the most accessible of all." We recommend visiting Fountain Acre Foods first. Take e xit 1 51 a nd travel north on US 27 about 7 miles and you'll see this emporium of everything Amish on the right side of the road at 1140 W Whitewater Road, Fountain City, IN 47341, phone 765-847-1897. Started by Stevie and Mary Ann Miller in 2007, this store has grown from a tiny bulk food outlet to a sprawling bakery, bulk food, cheese, and furniture emporium. If you are lucky enough to stop by **on** a Thursday, Friday, or Saturday you'll get in on some of the bakery's fresh doughnuts including specialties like caramel-glazed, peanut butter crème filled, and classic glazed. Succulent

IMPORTANT AT-A-GLANCE INFORMATION

AFFILIATION: Old Order Amish (Lancaster County, Pennsylvania affiliation)

shoofly pies, thickly frosted cakes, crusty baked breads, and plenty of other goodies beckon. A deli makes made-to-order sandwiches and twice-a-year cheese sales draw plenty of crowds. Be sure to sign up for the store's quarterly newsletter. The hand-written letter from Stevie is like receiving a note from a friend and gives all the store's latest happenings.

The Amish of Wayne County arrived here from Lancaster County where farmland prices had become nosebleed high. However, they still maintain very close ties with their brethren in Pennsylvania. Unlike most buggies in the Midwest, the Amish of Wayne County have distinctive gray-topped buggies and the women here wear a distinctive twin-peaked kapp.

Practically across the street at 1883 New Garden Road, Fountain City, IN 47341, phone 765-847-5003, is Miller's Dry Goods. This is a typical Lancaster County, Pennsylvania-type sundry offering everything from clothing to kitchen utensils.

For something a little simpler during the spring, summer, and fall, take exit 149B to US 35 and travel about 12 miles to Zook's produce stand. They sell great fresh produce. We've bought strawberries and melons from this wonderful place a when we've been in the area..

Travel a bit farther north on US 35 and hang a left on Carlos Road. Three miles south at 8025 Carlos Road you'll find the Wayne County Produce Auction. Started in 2010 by Amish farmers looking for a local market for their produce the auction is now held three times a week April through October. The auction begins at 1 p.m. on Mondays and 10 a.m. on Wednesdays and Fridays. While many of the bidders are from grocery stores and markets, there is always a "retail table" where consumers can browse and buy. For the latest auction times, call 765-886-5498.

While visiting the auction browse the area where there are Amish-owned businesses like Country Side Greenhouse. During the peak of melon season we found an Amish family selling delicious cantaloupe for 25 cents a piece by the roadside. A one-room Amish school is just down the road from the auction house.

So if you don't know much about Amish culture and you find yourself passing through Indiana on I-70 and can spare an hour, you'll get a great primer here.

GRABILL, INDIANA

The Amish settlement outside of Grabill is often overlooked in favor of the large more touristy communities in nearby Lagrange and Shipshewana, Indiana and even nearby Berne. But the Grabill Amish settlement is worth exploring. First of all, it's very accessible, sitting right off of interstate 469 which wraps around the east side of Fort Wayne. While most large Amish communities are far from major metropolitan areas, the Grabill settlement practically rubs shoulders with Fort Wayne. In fact, we've seen buggies clattering into the busy, suburban Chapel Ridge shopping area on Fort Wayne's east side, a setting that one often doesn't see as host to buggies. Of course the proximity to a major city like Fort Wayne does present challenges to the more insular Amish. Holding off suburban sprawl is always an issue. Some of the Amish homes in the Grabill area resemble typical middle-American subdivision living: brick homes with manicured lawns.

IMPORTANT AT-A-GLANCE INFORMATION

AFFILIATION: Swiss Amish, Traditional

The signature event of the year is the Grabill Country Fair, held the first full weekend of September. It's a great time to visit and get fresh kettle corn and apple butter.

Grabill Country Sales, 13813 Fairview Drive (phone 260-627-8330), is an interesting store that is a combination conventional grocery store and Amish bulk food store.

Another interesting stop in Grabill is Katie's Amish Dolls, 13312 Schwartz Rd. Call 260-627-8352 for hours. This home-based business is one of the few that we've run into that specialize in collectible Amish faceless dolls. The dolls are carefully crafted and pieced by Kathryn "Katie" Lengacher and her five daughters. Katie's also sells a variety of other hand-crafted items and furniture.

While Grabill retains a quirky country charm, plans are under way to transform the town into a more tourist-friendly destination.

The first phase of the tourist attraction has already been completed: Local store, Grabill Country Sales. The next phase is a 34-room hotel (Schlafenhaus) and family-style restaurant (Essenhaus) complex called the Grabillhaus. Early reports state the restaurant will feature Amish cooking and seat 360 people. These will be the cornerstones of a $50 million 9-phase project that promises to bring an indoor water park, dinner theater, flea market, stagecoach restaurant, trails, and senior living facility to the area. So if you're looking for the quaint charm of Grabill, you might want to visit now. We at *The Williams Guide* are generally not big fans of these sprawling tourist type enterprises, preferring instead home-based Amish businesses and quaint shops. However, this mega-project does boast the participation and investment of some area Amish so it'll be interesting to watch this unfold. Watch future editions of *The Williams Guide* for more updates.

WHAT'S IN A NAME?

Lots if you're Amish. Some surnames are universally common among the Old Order Amish. Yoders and Millers can be found in virtually every Amish settlement. But in Grabill a common last name among the Amish is Lengacher. That's not a name you see in many other Amish communities. In Lancaster County, Pennsylvania, Kings and Glicks are common, yet virtually unseen elsewhere. In Berne and Grabill, Indiana, Schwartzes and Grabers are quite common, a reflection of the area's Swiss lineage. There have also been various splits over the years within the Amish church, for instance, the Beachy Amish. For instance, the Beachy Amish. Yet don't assume that just because someone has the last name Beachy that they are Beachy, because there are many Beachy Amish who are Old Order. And don't assume an Amish person with the last name of Swartzentruber is Swartzentruber Amish because chances are they are Old Order.

MILROY, INDIANA

This is a quiet, quirky, unassuming Amish settlement about 20 minutes off of I-74 in rural southeastern Indiana.

This is a settlement we've been to on a couple of occasions. One was a frigid early winter day when the first snow sprinkled the fields. We were struck by just how flat, not Indiana-flat, but Kansas-flat, the area is. As if Milroy were an ironing board and the area had been pressed. The Amish settlement here is relatively small, but Troyer's Country Store, 10599 State Road 3, is a great example of a typical Amish sundry shop, selling everything from bolts of fabric to baked goods. Their phone number is (765) 629-2604.

Milroy is also home to Amish man Daniel Stutzman a renowned horse trainer who participates in equine clinics across the USA.

IMPORTANT AT-A-GLANCE INFORMATION

AFFILIATION: Swiss Amish

NORTHERN INDIANA

NORTHERN INDIANA

IMPORTANT AT-A-GLANCE INFORMATION

AFFILIATION: Old Order Amish; German Baptist Brethren, and Old Order Mennonite

LODGING: Plenty of bed and breakfasts in the area, plus some chain motels in Shipshewana and, if you prefer the amenities of bigger cities, Goshen, Elkhart, and South Bend are all close.

PROVISIONS: For a full service supermarket and pharmacy we love Martin's Super Market, a well-run regional chain. Location in northern Indiana Amish country at 242 N. Oakland Ave.

FOOD: There are plenty of dining options available, Amish and otherwise. The Blue Gate, 195 N Van Buren Street, Shipshewana, IN 46565, phone 888-447-4725, and Essen Haus, 240 US 20, Middlebury, IN 46540, phone 800-455-9471, are both huge tourist draws with their Amish style food offerings.

GETTING THERE: From Chicago: Interstate 80 (Toll road) East to exit 107 (Middlebury /Constantine). Turn right (South) onto State Road 13.

From Indianapolis: Take Interstate 69 North to US 20, Exit 148 (Lagrange). West on US 20 approximately 33 miles to SR 5. Right (North) on SR 5 about 2 miles to Division Street.

From Detroit, take Interstate 69 South to exit 148 (LaGrange), Merge onto US 20 W for approximately 33 miles, turn right onto East County Line Rd.

OTHER AREA ATTRACTIONS: The University of Notre Dame with its picturesque campus and storied athletics are just 30 minutes away in South Bend, 112 N Notre Dame Ave. Goshen College, 1700 S Main

Street, Goshen, also has a superb Mennonite Historical Library for researchers.

EDITOR'S CHOICE: Mullet's Fine Dining, Pathway Bookstore, E & S Sales, for lodging we recommend Blue Gate Garden Inn.

BRIEFLY

The settlements of northern Indiana comprise the third-largest Amish community in the world. Over 200 Amish, Old Order Mennonite, and German Baptist congregations spread out like a patchwork quilt over the farmlands south and east of the South Bend-Elkhart-Goshen metroplex. The whole area straddling the Michigan-Indiana border is known regionally as "Michiana."

HISTORY AND INDEPTH INFORMATION

The Amish first settled in northern Indiana after the Civil War when it was a remote rural outpost far from anywhere. Today it's still far from anywhere but a burgeoning Amish population has made the area the world's third largest Amish settlement in the world.

The northern Indiana Amish have grown and evolved in culturally distinct ways from other settlements elsewhere. The fortunes of the Amish have largely been tied to the area's ubiquitous RV industry. In 1934 the first trailer business set up shop in Elkhart. By the time the nation's post-war middle class economic expansion began in earnest in 1949, northern Indiana was a hub for everything trailer. Around the same time the rural largely agrarian Amish settlements were beginning to run out of land for their growing families. Also, farming was becoming less economically viable as inflation took off. All the while the RV factories continued to expand. The need for workers was never greater and the Amish provided a steady, willing, and able labor pool. An added bonus for factory management: the Amish didn't believe in joining unions so costs were held down. The Amish in northern Indiana largely developed into a factory-dependent culture. Much of that culture came crashing down during the Great Recession of 2007, forcing many Amish into home-based businesses such as greenhouses and cabinetry. As the economy has recovered, however, the RV factories have been hiring, once again tying the Amish in the area inextricably to the business.

Of course, not all the Amish here work in the RV business, there are still plenty of places to partake in the peace and quietude of Plain life. We'll share with you some of our favorite people and places in northern Indiana's Plain community. There are, by the way, other Plain groups in northern Indiana including Old Order Mennonites and Old German Baptist Brethren. Old Order Mennonites can best be distinguished from Amish by observing the adult males. Baptized adult men are clean-shaven unlike the Amish who sport beards.

FOR STARTERS….

If you're looking for a holistic, well-rounded Amish experience we recommend that your first stop be Menno-Hof, 510 S Van Buren Street, Shipshewana, IN 46565, phone 260-768-4117. This is a non-profit museum/cultural center devoted to telling and sharing the Anabaptist history. We like the non-profit nature of the facility and the fact that there are at least two Old Order Amish serving on the board of directors of the center. We visited this unique sharing center for the first time in the early 1990s not long after it opened and were impressed then, but their offerings and reach have only grown. Nestled on beautifully kept grounds, the facility was built by Amish and Mennonite craftsmen in a traditional barn-raising. But while the building was constructed the old-fashioned way, the museum is a high-tech homage to everything Amish. Multimedia presentations, interpretations, and colorful displays take the visitor on a fascinating journey spanning centuries. Explore a 17th century sailing ship and replicas of a 19th century print shop, meeting house, and Amish home.

THE STRING OF PEARLS

We call these towns the string of pearls because they are laced around Michiana gracefully like a necklace. LaGrange County, Indiana will likely become the second "majority Amish" county in the USA within the next decade, the first being Holmes County, Ohio. The largest concentrations of Amish are centered around the towns of Middlebury, LaGrange, Nappanee, Topeka, and perhaps the best known of them all, Shipshewana. Academics who study Amish culture sometimes put Nappanee in a separate settlement and they are, but for the purposes of this book we are including them with the other communities. If you could only visit one pearl in the string, we recommend Shipshewana and that is where we'll start.

SHIPSHEWANA

Amish beauty is in the eye of the beholder in Shipshewana or "Ship" as it is affectionately called by visitors. Some people visit Shipshewana and barely brush against Amish culture. They'll visit the famous flea market, perhaps take in a play at The Blue Gate, and then spend the evening in a nice hotel. To each their own. But we prefer to indulge in the incredible and authentic Amish ambiance this town offers. Here are some of our favorite stops.

E & S SALES: If you find yourself breezing through town and you could only make one stop, we recommend making this your destination. Almost every Amish community has a bulk food store where homemakers can stock up on staples, but E & S is like a bulk food store, pardon us, on steroids. Some locals jokingly call it the "Amish Costco." It's huge! In some ways we miss the quaint, smaller shop with their hissing gas lights and more crowded quarters. Bigger isn't necessarily better, but E & S has done a good job managing their growth. It's still a special store. The owners are Amish and it's amazing the efficiency in which they run the place without some of the electronic aids other businesses have.

Not only is this an Amish-owned business (which we prefer) many of their customers are Amish or Mennonite. Sometimes Plain people outnumber English, and buggies crowd out the cars. But one thing is for sure: E & S is always crowded. Crowded is not a bad thing, it gives the store a fun, energetic atmosphere and check-out lanes are usually speedy and well staffed. The fact that so many locals shop at the store is a sign that E & S is a gem of a bulk food store and not a tourist trap. The store practically doubled in size recently and their aisles are stocked with everything from difficult to find cookbooks to candies of all stripes. There is locally grown produce, breads of all types, and a myriad of mixes from soup bases to cakes. We've seen over two dozen types of flour gracing the shelves. Some of the merchandise reflects the changing culinary culture of the Amish. A whole shelf is devoted to olive oil, a more favored frying flavor these days than the traditional lard (although they do sell that also). They do brisk business among Amish homemakers who need to buy 20 pound sacks of flour and 50 pounds of sugar, but the place is equally appealing for someone who just needs to buy for a small family. E & S is the "king" of the bulk food stores, a massive emporium of spices, snacks, cheeses, candies, cookbooks, and almost anything else one would need to feed an army. We like to buy horns of Colby cheese here. You can freeze cheese, by the way.

Their phone number and address is 260-768-4736, 1265 N State Road 5, Shipshewana, IN 46565. Open Monday through Friday, 7:30 a.m. to 5:30 p.m., and Saturdays until 4 p.m.

GREEN MEADOW HOUSES 0725N 840W, Shipshewana, IN 46565, 260-768-7863, ext. 1. Talking about milking peoples' interest in birds! This is an offbeat business owned by Amish entrepreneur John Hochstetler. He makes his birdhouses from polywood which is made from melted milk jugs and pressed into planks. A visit to his store provides a panoply of hand-made, eco-friendly bird-houses and bird-feeders. Definitely a unique store and worth a visit for bird enthusiasts.

CREEKSIDE BOOK STORE & FABRIC, 3650 N State Road 5 – This is an Amish-owned bookstore in the town of Shipshewana. The store is operated by Chris Miller, a deacon in the Amish church. The store primarily caters to Amish customers. Peruse the many titles on hand and enjoy the Amish ambiance.

YODER'S HOME-STYLE COOKING,10525 W 325 N, Shipshewana, IN. 260-768-3078We really like this dining option because it is held in an Amish home and served in the deep tradition of Plain cooking. Here's the tough part about dining at Yoder's: you MUST make a reservation. If it's just your family of four wanting a home-cooked meal on an Amish farm you may be out of luck. But not necessarily. If another group is scheduled for the same night you can piggyback onto their evening. The Yoder's meal is billed as a Thresher's meal, a hearty harvest feast with fork tender roast beef, farm-raised chicken with a hint of crispy breading, and lettuce-cauliflower-broccoli salad served alongside soft-as-cotton homemade bread slathered with Amish "wedding spread", a confection of peanut butter, marshmallow fluff,and corn syrup. And for dessert: plenty of pie, whether it be the creamy chocolate, the crisp harvest apple, or the peanut butter pie whipped to a perfection confection. Again, you must make a reservation, be flexible, and you'll be rewarded with a wonderful meal steeped in Amish tradition and culinary culture.

B & L WOODCRAFTS, 10045 W. 250 North: We like this store because most of the hand-made furniture is made on site by Amish owner Lyle Helmuth. Play-houses, swing-sets, and other eco-friendly furniture is the specialty of B & L. Their store, located at the Helmuth homestead, is located a couple of miles west of Shipshewana.

Farming Days

Held on the final Friday and Saturday in July, we really like this event because it is held on an actual Old Order Amish farm and is run by an Amish husband and wife who have a genuine and deep devotion to preserving their culture's vanishing agrarian roots. You can't beat the $5 admission price for all that you get, including an invitation to camp on the three acres of field they have set aside for visitors. Merv and Edna Yoder, 6450 W 275 N, Shipshewana, IN 46565, phone 260-768-4986, began this event back in 2004 as just a small farming demonstration given to neighbors and friends. Marv explained to us that he didn't want the agrarian roots of the Amish to be lost, especially with so many Amish in northern Indiana working in factories. It's an entire day dedicated to showcasing Amish agrarianism on a working Amish farm. Food is always a great way to experience Amish culture and we love this event because the Saturday lunch is provided by Shipshewana Meadows Schools, an Amish parochial school. There just aren't too many events like this, so we highly recommend it.

Tip

DRIVING IN NORTHERN INDIANA

This area contains one of the largest concentrations of horse-drawn vehicles anywhere. The Amish here are also permitted to ride bicycles. Because the area is so flat it can be easy to lull oneself into a false sense of security, be alert for slow-moving vehicles of all types.

While you'll see plenty of Amish buggies almost anywhere you go in northern Indiana, one of our favorite drives between Middlebury and Shipshewana is Road 250 N. The road goes right through the heart of the area's Amish community so you'll be greeted to postcard scenes of laundry on the line, men working in the fields, and plenty of home-based businesses.

LAGRANGE

PATHWAY   BOOKSTORE:
2580N 250 W in LaGrange. This might be the "Amish Barnes & Noble" stocked with hundreds of titles that appeal to an Amish audience, but non-Amish are welcome to stop by and browse also. No jazz music, coffee-bar, or big comfy chairs to sit in, but this unassuming book nook tucked away in northern Indiana's Amish country will please bibliophiles of all stripes.

DID YOU KNOW?

One of the ways the Old Order Amish stay tethered to their simpler, slower pace is by refusing to own automobiles.   Notice the word is refuse to own, not use. There is a distinct difference in the two terms.   The Amish fear that owning automobiles would tear apart the fabric of family life in much the same way it has non-Amish America.   By refusing to own cars, the Amish are making a statement about community and connection.   Churches stay close-knit geographically because everyone needs to live close to one another when buggy is your main mode of transport. Like with many technologies, however, the Amish have made compromises to adapt to the changing world around them.   The reality is that to attend a wedding or funeral faraway, horse-and-buggy is impractical. So the Amish will hire non-Amish drivers to take them.

NAPPANEE-BREMEN

The Amish community around Bremen is nicknamed "Rentown". The Amish who moved to the area in the 1960s began christening it "Rentown" after an old Pennsylvania Dutch word *(rum-runna)* and the restless souls who first moved here who had a penchant for roaming and exploring. Anyway, the name stuck and today several Amish businesses make up Rentown. There are several ways to enjoy this area. We highly recommend attending the annual Rentown Garden Walk and Bake Sale. This event is held the second Saturday of June from 9 a.m. to 3 p.m. All proceeds generated go to Rolling Meadow School, an Amish parochial school in the community. The Amish participate in all aspects of the event, so there's a wonderful chance to mix and mingle and immerse oneself in Plain culture.

Show up at the Rolling Meadow School anytime during the event so you can register. There you can sample fresh brewed mint tea from area gardens, homemade doughnuts, and tour the Amish school. There is also an all-day bake sale at the school where anything from scratch-made bread to egg noodles are for sale. Amish volunteers will have maps available to area homes participating in the garden walk. Usually about 8 to 12 families volunteer to showing the way open their gardens up to participants in the tour. You can visit the homes and learn about flower, produce, or vegetable gardening. Some Amish even serve baked goods or other fare to visitors on the tour. One home offered helpings of a homemade, hearty stew cooked in an iron kettle to visitors.

Each year features one "signature event" of a large scale. One year featured a barn tour where visitors could learn up close about farm animals. Another year offered a "maple syrup camp" to learn about sugaring.

Other than visiting home-based businesses (a wonderful way to experience Plain culture), the Amish remain a pretty insular group, so to be able to attend an event where the Amish open their farmsteads to outsiders is extraordinary. The event was inspired by similar tours held in cities across the country.

Naomi Troyer, the Amish woman who initially thought of this idea to fundraise for the school, had attended the nearby South Bend Garden Walk and was impressed, she told the local Pilot News newspaper.

When reflecting on her visits to the gardens in South Bend, she thought, "You know what? We can do that."

There is no charge to attend the event, but visitors are asked to register and donate.

RENTOWN COUNTRY STORE, 1533 3rd Rd, is a great reason to visit Rentown. The store offers over 50 varieties of cheeses, bulk foods, and bakery items. But we like Rentown Country Store because of the homemade, scratch-made food items offered from what they call the "Snack Den." The Snack Den is open from 8 a.m. to 2 pm. There are only a few tables and it's not really a restaurant per se, but they do have a menu you can order off of that includes rib-sticking favorites like biscuits and gravy, pancakes, ham and eggs, baked oatmeal, French toast, and pie. There simply aren't many opportunities to directly experience Amish culinary culture and this is one place where you can. The Rentown Country Store is open Mondays through Fridays 8 a.m. to 6 p.m. and Saturdays from 8 a.m. to 5 p.m. The store accepts cash, check, and credit cards. To learn more call 574-546-9010.

BURKHOLDER'S COUNTRY STORE: 29999 County Road 56, Nappanee, IN 46550, phone 574-773-4279. Larry and Marlene Burkholder are the pleasant proprietors of this comfortingly typical Amish variety store.

MILLER'S VARIETY STORE, 8920 N State Route 19, Etna Green, IN 46524, phone 574-646-2000. This is another Amish variety store, but they seem to have an emphasis on kitchenwares.

While there are plenty of places to chow down on Amish-style food in Northern Indiana, our favorite places are the ones that you have to look a little harder to find. For Example:

MULLET'S: There are Old Order Amish who do open their homes for meals for visitors. Merlin and Mary Lou Mullet and their seven children serve homemade rolls with fresh from the orchard apple butter and tender chicken that hangs for dear life to the bone. You'll get to enjoy the meal in an Amish home, surrounded by the simple serenity and authentic ambiance that makes this lifestyle so appealing to many. The Mullet's usually serve groups of 10 or more, but you may be able to get lumped in with another group. So prepare to eat family style and make some new friends. Leave them a voicemail at 574-773-2140 or visit them at 72280 County Road 100N in Nappanee, IN 46550. Prices are subject to change, but a whole meal including dessert runs $16.50.

MIDDLEBURY

COUNTRY LANE BAKERY, 59162 County Road 43, Middlebury, IN 46540, phone 574-825-7918. This is an Amish-owned and operated bakery. Howard and Ida Yoder run this small but popular place from their home. The Yoder's bakery is legendary for their whole-grain yeast breads, caramel slathered cinnamon rolls (iced to order), and 3 dozen pie varieties for custom order. A selection of whoopie pies also are customer favorites. Call ahead to place a large custom order. This bakery also gets our "early bird" award. We've never encountered an Amish bakery that opens each day at 5 a.m. They close at 4 p.m. and 2 p.m. on Saturdays. Country Lane is closed on Mondays.

RISE N ROLL: While we prefer to highlight Amish and Plain-owned businesses in this book, Rise N Roll Bakery's recent Amish roots and fervent fans merit a mention in this book. Old Order Amish husband and wife Viola and Orvin Bontranger started selling homemade doughnuts from their front porch in Middlebury.

Their baked goods developed such a following that they eventually opened their own bakery next to their home. Fans of Rise N Roll continued to clamor for their confections so eventually a new facility was built. Rise N Roll is now at the corner of 1150 W. and U.S. 20, just into LaGrange County and 3 miles west of Shipshewana at 1065 N 1150 W, Middlebury, IN 46540, phone 574-825-4032.

Each Amish bakery has their specialty. And while you can't go wrong with anything you order here, their cinnamon caramel doughnuts are mouth-wateringly amazing and are what first put them on the map. The recipe is one that has been in Orvin's family for some time. The bakery also offers a popular crunch candy as well as deli meats and cheeses, made-to-order sandwiches and pizza.

The bakery was sold in 2009 just before they moved to their current location. The owners are non-Amish investors who live locally and the products are growing so popular that Rise N Roll franchise locations are planned in the Michiana area. We always worry about growth severing the product from its original charm and watering down the culinary quality. On a recent visit, however, we found the food quality still amazing and the Amish involvement evident at every level. Original owners Orvin and Viola are still at the bakery every day and it shows. We'll hope Rise N Roll stays true to its roots as it grows.

DUTCH COUNTRY MARKET, 11401 CR 1, Middlebury: We place a premium in this guide on Amish-owned businesses and Amish-owned businesses that are run out of the farmstead are our favorite, which is why we love the Dutch Country Market. This quaint, but busy, farmstop is run by Katie and Norman Lehman. The Lehman's are perhaps best known for their noodles, handcrafted with care using an old favorite recipe. The Lehmans can churn out close to 50,000 pounds of noodles of varying thicknesses in a year. The ones that seem most popular are the extra thick eat-with-a-fork noodles. The Lehman's six children help out running the market and making the noodles. The Lehman's also make 36,000 pounds of homemade honey each year from their own hives which is then sold as one of nine different flavors of honey, balms, or soaps. Some of the honey is pasteurized, while other batches are not. Norman Lehman says it's possible since the honey's pollen is local that a teaspoon a day will ward off allergies, but we'll leave that verdict to people smarter than us to decide!

Getting Active

Getting active in Amish country is one of the best ways to see and experience it, whether it be running, biking, or walking. Guest writer Sarah McGaugh shares her running experience in Shipshewana.

Running In Shipshewana

By Sarah McGaugh

I packed my running clothes and running shoes in my carry-on as we made our way to Shipshewana, Indiana this past week. Caring for myself and attending to my health are gifts I give myself every day. Responsible calorie counting is also a part of who I am now. I can no sooner forget about that obligation to myself than I could forget one of my children at the airport.

Shipshewana would really be my first test of running while traveling. Sure, I counted in the Bay Area and in Idyllwild this past spring and winter, but I didn't take my running clothes. And Shipshewana is Amish country. Amish food is head-over-heels delicious and comforting and social. Amish peanut butter. Freshly baked bread. Fall apart beef roasts. Pie. Pie, pie, pie. Banana cream, chocolate mousse, cherry, peanut butter, shoo fly. Yep, a definite test.

At first I thought I would just roll out of bed and do the bare minimum (2 or 3 miles) and get on with all the other activities. Yet on that first morning of my run, I discovered something: this was a special time to explore the countryside and little town. Wherever I could run, I could go. Within a mile of that first morning, I never wanted to stop. I realized how much more intimately I could know this place by running it. The sounds, the scents, the changes in the morning sunlight, the pace of life: I could become part of these all just through being present in my run and letting my feet and body go as far as it could. How can I have never run in a new town before? Why did I not run on the beach in Hawaii? To know the streets, the byways, the details of a new place is to put it forever into my mind and heart. I know now that, no matter where I go in my travels, I will run it. I will run it, not just for exercise and my health, but also because it is through this effort on the land that I can make the place partly my own. I have never experienced more intimacy with a new place than I experienced on this trip.

I ran five mornings out of the six mornings we were there. I took Sunday morning off, out of respect and deference. Even so, by twilight on Sunday my mom and the kiddos and I took a three mile walk right before dinner. That was proper: as we walked past the Amish homes, many of the children were playing (hammock, volleyball, running games) while we could hear the adult chatter and merriment coming from shared dinners near kitchen windows. So really, I exercised each day.

My body woke up right at 6:00 AM every morning, and I would get up and look out at the sheep and cows grazing on the farm right outside our windows. The sun would just be coming up. The inn was quiet, my children still sleeping and husband, too. Then it was out the door and into the Indiana morning. Most of the mornings were misty and not quite cold but extremely pleasant, cooler than where I live. The last couple of mornings were humid even at 6:00 AM. There was nothing but a feeling of sheer joy and magic to be running in that mistiness, watching the sun break, saying good morning to the cows and hearing the horses neigh. Birds were everywhere—I didn't use my headphones and music. Almost no one else was awake, except for the Amish part of the community, and if I went far enough in the right places, I got to see some of the Amish already hard at work so early in the morning. Women were working in their gardens. Some would pass by in their buggies or on bicycles. I was one of the only "English" people up at that same time.

I would run past corn fields, beautiful in the light. In five mornings, I ran 26.08 miles. I didn't gain any weight on this trip (I weighed myself yesterday, the morning after we got back...and today, I weigh even less than yesterday). I tasted many delicious things, but never went overly crazy. I never once felt deprived. I budgeted calories in the morning at the inn's complimentary buffet and made choices about which food experiences I wanted more than others. I simply cannot eat it all, and that is okay with me. It's just reality. The first day I was there, I went out and bought packets of tea. Life is about the choices I make and understanding that I cannot pin those choices on anyone—or anything—else.

Running in Shipshewana was about honoring that promise to myself, but it became so much more than that. I felt so connected to the land and the people. I know the map of that town like the back of my own hand now. At night when I go to bed, I imagine running my various routes. My heart aches a bit for them. I wonder when my legs will run that place again. Shipshewana has a big piece of my essence right now.

On my last morning, I ran for over seven miles, connecting portions of my favorite routes and saying goodbye to every part I loved. I didn't want the run to end and wanted to go much further but I knew I had to get back to dress my children and finish packing.

I never knew what it could mean to run during a vacation. What began as a way to get my daily exercise has turned into a quest. Running has become so meditative for me, a way to be in tune with myself and my surroundings. I think about all I would have missed had I left my running shoes at home this time. Unthinkable. The memories I made while running are some of my most personal and favorite on this trip.

I know my legs will remember, too, and if we're ever there again, they will celebrate at the sight of their favorite paths.

Sarah McGaugh is a freelance editor and maintains a blog at **birdinyourhand.com** Essay reprinted with permission.

INDIANA

PARKE COUNTY

PARKE COUNTY, IN

Up until the early 1990s this area was known more for its storied covered bridges than its Amish. But after an influx arrived from Lancaster County in the mid-90s the area is now known for both. Today, 31 covered bridges grace the county's roads providing serene scenery and yesteryear nostalgia. There area's Amish presence is growing and may justify an expanded entry in future editions of this book. Some favorite stops include:

PEACHY'S BULK FOODS, 1631 Mull Rd, Rockville, IN, *phone 765-569-1080*. This is our Amish business in Parke County. This is a typical Amish bulk food store with assorted spices, flours, candies, and baked goods, such as breads, cookies, and whoopie pies.

ROCKVILLE PRODUCE AUCTION, 3300 N. 400, E Rockville, IN 47872, *phone 765-569-6840.* This is an auction started by Amish farmers to bring their produce to market. While the auction primarily caters to wholesalers, anyone is welcome to come. It is an Amish immersion experience watching the lots get sold off, hearing the cadence of the Amish auctioneers, watching straw hat-clad barefoot boys hauling loads of plants and veggies to people's cars. There is a flat rate table where small quantities of in-season produce is available for tourists or households to purchase. The auction schedule varies, but generally sales are held May through October, at 2 p.m. Mondays and 10 a.m. Wednesdays and Fridays. (Call ahead to confirm.)

DID YOU KNOW?

CHURCH STRUCTURE: Like snowflakes, no two Amish churches are alike. The Amish church lacks a central administrative structure like other churches have. The centralized structure of most churches whether it be the Mormons and their headquarters in Salt Lake City or Roman Catholics taking their direction from the Vatican, the highest authority in the Amish church is the LOCAL bishop. There is no "Amish Pope". So while most Amish churches share similarities in theology and tradition, one can also see wide variations. Some Amish churches permit indoor plumbing, while others do not. Most Amish prefer not to be photographed, but in some church districts the rules are more liberal and photography is permitted.

IOWA

Iowa has had an Amish population for well over a century, but for a long time the communities were clustered around Kalona, Hazleton, and Bloomfield. The large Amish birth rate and need for farmland elsewhere has caused the state's Plain population to spread out beyond its traditional areas. An Amish presence can now be found in most of the state.

BLOOMFIELD

The rural roads between the town of Drakesville and Bloomfield are home to one of the more entrepreneurial Amish settlements. While other Amish communities are larger and have far more home-based businesses, the Bloomfield settlement is not huge (around 185 families spread among eight church districts), yet there are over 90 home-based businesses selling everything from baked goods to buggies. Be sure to stop by the welcome center in Bloomfield, because they offer maps of area Amish businesses. The address is 301 N. Washington in Bloomfield.

IMPORTANT AT-A-GLANCE INFORMATION

AFFILIATION: Old Order Amish, Traditional

We love attending auctions because it's a fun, relaxed atmosphere where Amish and non-Amish interact. Each Tuesday and Friday the Southern Iowa Produce auction chatters to life. It's billed as Iowa's largest Amish auction and gives a market for local Amish green thumbs to peddle their homegrown wares. The auction is located at 19141 Ice Ave, Bloomfield, phone 641-722-3623 for more information. Most of the lots are geared towards wholesalers and retailers, but there are always some smaller lots for individuals who want some fresh garden goodies. There are also special auction days throughout the season, including a Mother's Day flower auction the Saturday before Mom's big day and a special fall crops (pumpkins, anyone?) auction. During peak season the auction runs three days week, starting at 4 p.m. on Mondays and 10 a.m. on Wednesdays and Fridays.

Other Amish businesses to check to out are listed here. (Be sure to use your GPS to find the stores, because even though the mailing address is Bloomfield, most of the stores are closer to Drakesville).

SHADY LANE VARIETY, Phone 641-664-0212, 16575 Jade Ave. Bloomfield. This is a classic Amish-owned "a little bit of everything store" offering everything from greeting cards to ice cream freezers. A visit here is a little bit like a treasure hunt!

GRABER'S COUNTRY STORE, 641-664-3163, 18932 200th Street, this is another "treasure hunt" store selling everything from Red Wing shoes to camping equipment.

THE BAKERY BARN, 19070 180th Street, Bloomfield, this Amish bakery is only open on Fridays and Saturdays so it is worth planning a stop here around your visit. They offer typical Amish baked goodies (pecan cinnamon rolls, anyone?) with some offbeat specialities like caramel apple pie and bumbleberry pie.

HERSHBERGER BULK FOODS, 18980 180th Street, We love this emporium of everything! If your cupboards are bare at home you can find anything here from fresh produce to baking ingredients and deli items. This is a classic Amish bulk food store.

YODER'S KOUNTRY KORNER, 21050 Ice Avenue, Bloomfield. There is a furniture side to this store which is open 6 days a week showcasing Amish furniture craftsmanship. On Fridays and Saturdays the "sweet side" opens up featuring homemade cinnamon rolls, cookies, pies, and local specialty, butterhorns.

Our final recommendation for Bloomfield is to enjoy the Amish Iowa ambiance by cruising the rural roads, enjoying the serene scenes of a simpler life. Many home-based businesses aren't always on the tourist maps, so a settlement like Bloomfield yields constant new discoveries!

YODER'S NATURAL FARM: Not all Amish farmers are organic. Organic farming, in fact, is a relatively recent trend among Amish farmers and nowhere is this exhibited better than Robert Yoder's Farm. Christened Yoder's Natural Farm, customers can purchase pasture-raised broilers and eggs, pastured grass-fed beef. Yoder's products are also sold at the Fairfield Farmer's Market in nearby Fairfield, Iowa on Wednesdays from 3:00 p.m. to 6:00 p.m. and on Saturday mornings from 8:00 a.m. - 1:00 p.m. The Farmer's Market is held during the summer atHoward Park at the corner of E. Grimes and S. Court Street.

Yoder describes his farming methods as "beyond organic." He described to us the way he raises his animals, creating a life for his livestock that is natural and humane, which in turn creates a healthier meat. Robert Yoder's farm is located at 19222 Jade Ave.

HAZLETON

IMPORTANT AT-A-GLANCE INFORMATION

AFFILIATION: Old Order Amish, conservative

LODGING: There are several motels 10 minutes away in Oelwein. While there are some bed and breakfasts in the area, we've not stayed in any to recommend. Watch future editions of this guide for updates!

PROVISIONS: Fareway Foods, 102 2nd Street SE, Oelwein, IA 50662, phone 319-283-2872, offers a range of groceries and supplies for planning a picnic in nearby Amish country.

FOOD: There are no Amish restaurants in the Hazleton settlement, but plenty of bakeries to fill up at and a deli or two to find a sandwich. Nearby Oelwein offers a variety of restaurants including the well-regarded Leo's Italian Restaurant, 29 South Frederick Avenue, Oelwein, IA 50662, phone 319-283-1655, for those who want to balance out a day of eating whoopee pies and Amish cookies.

GETTING THERE: From the south take Iowa interstate 380 to Cedar

Rapids to the interchange with Iowa State Route 150.   Take 150 north to Oelwein.

OTHER ATTRACTIONS: Northeast Iowa's "bluff country" offers much to an outdoor enthusiast.

BRIEFLY

The Hazleton community is home to northeast Iowa's largest Amish community.

INDEPTH AND HISTORY

The first Amish settled in the area in 1914, coming from the more progressive community of Kalona (see page 87). The hope was that the Hazleton settlement could hew to the church's more traditional, agrarian, rural roots and that vision has held fast to this day.

The Hazleton, Iowa community made headlines in the 1960s as one of the flashpoints in the Amish battle to maintain their own parochial schools. The issue had been a contentious one for some time and not just in Iowa. Similar clashes were playing out in Wisconsin's Amish community and among Old Order Mennonites in the Dayton, Virginia community. The Amish, for religious and cultural reasons, wanted to limit education to the eighth grade. They maintained that for an Amish life the children only needed to attend eight grades, after that the children would learn all they would need working side by side with family on the farm and in their shops. There were other reasons. The 1960s were a time when rural school systems were beginning to consolidate and the cultural influence of the "hippie movement" was beginning to trickle into public school systems. Religion's influence was also on the wane in public schools. All of these factors were threatening to upend the Amish way of life. Their answer: parochial schools, the traditional "one room" schoolhouses of Little House on the Prairie fame. But the governor and the state legislature weren't having any of it. In November 1965 when armed police officers and public school officials arrived at Amish school Number 1, this what happened according to the Associated Press:

With their weeping mothers and flabbergasted school officials looking on, 14 Amish school children bolted into a cornfield behind their rural one-room school and hid yesterday to avoid going to city school. The children broke into a run for a nearby cornfield. The boys, dressed in their knickers and with their traditional broad-brimmed hats firmly on their heads, jumped a fence and disappeared. The Amish girls, clothed in ankle-length gowns and with bonnets on their heads, also eluded the pursuing officers.

The raid became a public relations disaster for the governor as pictures of weeping Amish mothers were published in newspapers across the world. The legislature and government agreed to a compromise that would allow the Amish to attend their own schools, but the push for federal rules would continue for another 7 years.

Today, things are quieter in Buchanan County. The one-room school still stands and the settlement remains one of the more conservative ones. The bulk of the Amish settlement in the area is to the west of Hazleton and we recommend just driving and exploring the grid of rural roads in the area.

PLAINVIEW COUNTRY STORE, 1146 Fairbank-Amish Blvd, Hazleton, IA 50641, phone 319-342-1000. A classic Amish bulk food store offering everything from cookbooks to candies and flour to baked goods.

STUTZMAN'S BUGGY SHOP, 1273 Fairbank-Amish Blvd, Hazleton, IA 50641. Admittedly most non-Amish don't have a real need to go into a buggy shop, but Leroy Stutzman's business on Amish Boulevard specializes in fixing and making brand new buggies and as long as you are respectful of his time, visitors are welcome!

Amish Boulevard

Use Iowa Road W13 as your north-south orientation to discover a whole range of Amish businesses. This road is known locally as "Amish Boulevard", with that being the official mailing address of those who live on the road. Over 50 Amish-owned businesses from bakeries and bulk foods to harness shops line Amish Boulevard. Most are open 8 a.m. to 5 p.m.

There's also plenty to explore off of Amish Boulevard and we would encourage visitors to do just that. You'll find gems like Whispering Pines Bakery, 1407 145th Street, Fairbank, IA 50629. Viola only opens her bakery on Friday and Saturdays from 8 a.m. to 5 a.m. and she's legendary for her melt-in-your-mouth sweet rolls.

DAY TRIPP

In 2010 the tiny town of Tripp, South Dakota, about an hour or so from the northwestern tip of Iowa, generated quite a bit of excitement. Until then the state had no Amish presence. All of that changed when several families moved to the area from Tomah, Wisconsin's increasingly crowded Amish community

Amish communities don't always succeed. Amish author David Luthy chronicles this phenoma in his book *Settlements that Failed* (Pathway Publishing). As of his writing, the Tripp community appears to be hanging on and we hear reports that one Amish woman holds weekly bake sales. Stay tuned to future editions of The Williams Guide for updates on Tripp.

KALONA

IMPORTANT AT-A-GLANCE INFORMATION

AFFILIATION: Old Order Amish, traditional

LODGING: There are plenty of chain motels in nearby Iowa City. There are some bed and breakfasts in the Kalona area but we have not stayed in any to recommend, stay tuned to future revised editions of this book for updates or visit **www. thewilliamsguide.com**

PROVISIONS: Hy-Vee is a regional supermarket chain which we like, there are several locations in Iowa City. The one at 1720 Waterfront Drive, Iowa City 52240, phone 319-354-7601, is closest to the Amish community and offers a full-line of picnic items and supplies from buns to batteries.

FOOD: There are plenty of wonderful restaurants in Iowa City, from Thai to traditional American. In Kalona, try Kalona Family Restaurant, 111 5th Street, Kalona, IA 52247, phone 319-656-2277, for basic diner fare. There also are some wonderful dining options

15 minutes away in Wellman at the Riverside Casino and Golf Resort.

GETTING THERE: From Iowa City and Interstate 80 take Iowa Highway One south 20 miles to the Kalona community.

OTHER ATTRACTIONS: Iowa City offers amenities that you'd usually only find in much larger cities because of it being home to the University of Iowa.

BRIEFLY

The Kalona, Iowa Amish settlement is one of the largest and oldest west of the Mississippi River. With their liberal use of motorized tractors, this group is one of the more progressive Amish communities.

HISTORY AND INDEPTH

The gently rolling fields of southeast Iowa can't really compare to other Amish settlements for sheer beauty, but there is a sense of history one soaks in when visiting this unique community.

The Amish first settled in the Kalona area in 1846 and for a number of years this was one of the most prominent communities west of the Mississippi. In 1987, People Magazine ran an article about the abundance of Millers and Yoders in the community and how all the similar names gave the local mailman fits.   The article recounts:

"This isn't like a regular office you go into and memorize names," said postmaster Terry Hagedorn, with some understatement. "It's trickier."

There are 17 Mary Millers in the Kalona area. Five Marlin Millers. Seven Barbara Millers. Twelve Mary Yoders. Five John Yoders. There is an L. David Yoder and a David L. Yoder. There are Alta and Alva Yoders and Vera, Verba and Verda Millers. There was a Miller Yoder, but he moved away.

In that same article, Kalona is called "the largest Amish community" west of the Mississippi. That distinction probably now is held by Jamesport, Missouri or even Webster County in the Show-Me-State. But Kalona's Amish community does roll out the welcome mat for visitors with a variety of businesses. The names seem a little more creative here. No "Emma's Bakery" or "Yoder's Pastry" here. The Golden Delight Bakery, 2289 Johnson-Washington Rd, Kalona, IA 52247, is an Amish-owned bakery. And it is for the early birds, opening each day at 7 a.m. and staying open until 5 p.m. This bakery is known for its homemade pies, breads, and hot glazed doughnuts. Buy some doughnuts and then sit outside at one of their picnic tables and enjoy the surrounding Amish ambiance.

STRINGTOWN DRY GOODS (no one seems to know where the name comes from), 2266 540th Street, Kalona, Iowa 52247, is a bulk food and produce store that lures people from the collegiate enclave of Iowa City into the country side with their seasonal assortments from homegrown onions in the spring to apple cider and pumpkin butter in the fall. Ready to eat homemade granola, bulk oatmeal, cheeses, and noodles, most locally made, can also be found.

KALONA CHEESE: Known by its local name as simply "The Cheese Haus", 2206 540th Street SW, Kalona, Iowa 52247, phone 319-656-2776, this is a popular stop for those visiting the Kalona Amish settlement. Although the cheese facility is not owned by Amish or Mennonites, there are Plain workers there and much of their milk comes from nearby Amish farms. The Cheese Haus is located right in the heart of the Amish settlement so you'll see a lot of buggies and well-kept farms en route.

The Cheese Haus stocks over 200 kinds of cheese in their retail store where customers can also watch the cheese being made through observation windows. And for those who love cheese curds, Kalona Cheese is one of very few places in the country where customers can purchase fresh cheese curds that are made daily. In addition to cheese, the store also carries a variety of gourmet foods including meats, teas, jams, mustards, candies, and other hard to find items. Gift packages are shipped all over the United States.

Visiting an Amish settlement is already in some ways like a step back in time, but take a step even farther back by visiting the Kalona Historical Village, 715 D Avenue, Kalona, IA 52247, phone 319-656-3232. Here you'll find a pristinely restored village almost exactly as it was in the mid-1800s when this was still wild and woolly frontier country. There is also a rich repository of documents and artifacts tying into the area's Amish and Mennonite history, a sort of museum within a museum.

The Kalona Historical Village is also host of the annual "autumn festival" held the final weekend of September. The day includes old time demonstrations of homemade apple butter making, cornmeal grinding, broom making, hay baling and blacksmithing. Admission to the festival is $5 for adults, $2 for children.

We recommend staying in Iowa City and enjoying the youth and energy of the quintessential college town before stealing away for the day among the Amish.

DAY TRIP –
THE AMANA
COLONIES

We hear people referring often to the Amana Colonies as "Amish" or something similar to the Amish. There is, however, no connection between the two. Theologically and historically they have more in common with the German Baptists (see page 11) and lifestyle-wise they enjoy more similarities to the Hutterites. Still, for those interested in Plain and communal cultures, a visit to the Amana Colonies would be worthwhile.

We recommend using Iowa City as your base to explore the Kalona Amish settlement and the Amana Colonies.

For over 80 years Pietist, a German religious group lived almost entirely self-sufficiently in a remote tract of Iowa fields. The group, which peaked at over 1,800 residents in the 1880s were products of a 19th century Utopian movement. Societies were created to try to smooth the creases of capitalism and create more just lives. During the heyday of the Amana Colonies the industrious residents farmed, invented, and built innovative industries that last to this day. Amana refrigerators were developed by a colony member and a factory was started to churn them out. In 1947, Amana manufactured the first upright freezer for the home, and in 1949 it added a side-by-side refrigerator/freezer.   The brand lives to this day as a subsidiary of Whirlpool. The communal aspect of the Amana Colonies ended in the 1930s as more and more members chafed under the lack of individual freedom. The businesses of the colony were spun off into a separate corporation which today still operates. Many descendants of the commune dwellers remain today and church services are still held. Original buildings have been restored and the colonies welcome visitors to explore and dine in some of their restaurants. Colony restaurants are known for their heaping portions, family style meals, and made from scratch cooking. The Colony Inn Restaurant, in existence since 1860 in one form or another, is the oldest eatery. It is located at 741 47th Avenue, Amana, Iowa 52203, phone 319-622-3030.

GETTING THERE: From Interstate 80, take Exit 225, turning north on Hwy 151. Travel along Hwy 151 for five miles until you reach the intersection of Hwy 151 and Hwy 6. Turn left on Hwy 6 to go to South Amana, West Amana and High Amana. Turn right to go to Homestead, Amana or Middle Amana. The Amana Colonies Trail, Hwy 220, is a 17-mile loop that connects all seven villages.

The Amana Colonies Visitors Center is located in the village of Amana, 622 46th Avenue, Amana, IA 52203, phone 800-579-2294, in a restored corn crib. The Visitors Center is your first stop for information about the Amana Colonies providing Visitors Guides, maps and brochures for area businesses. Menus for all Amana Colonies restaurants are also provided.

KANSAS

Kansas has seen its Amish and Mennonite population grow over the past decade. For most of the 1900s the frontier feel town of Yoder, outside of Hutchinson, was the western most Amish community. There has also been an Amish presence near Garnett outside of Kansas City. But recent years have seen Amish settlements established near Axtell in the north-central part of the state and throughout the wide swaths of rural southeastern Kansas. The Yoder community is still the "Amish Capital of Kansas" and that is the area we focus on in this section.

YODER/ PARTRIDGE

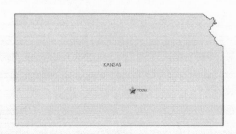

FOOD: Carriage Crossing Restaurant, 10002 S. Yoder Road, Yoder, KS 67585, phone 620-465-3612, offers a full range of traditional American fare and an outstanding selection of pies.

GETTING THERE: From Wichita take State Route 96 north to the Yoder Road exit.

IMPORTANT AT-A-GLANCE INFORMATION

AFFILIATION: Yoder - Old Order Amish, traditional. Partridge - Old Order Amish, progressive; Beachy Amish Mennonite.

LODGING: Plenty of chain motels in nearby Hutchinson and Wichita. Sunflower Inn Bed & Breakfast, 3307 Switzer Road, Yoder, KS 67585, phone 620-465-2000 (see Editor's Choice).

PROVISIONS: A Dillon's Grocery Store, 1321 N. Main Street, Hutchinson, KS 67501, phone 620-662-1273, and numerous other chain stores population the east side of Hutchinson, about 20 minutes from Yoder.

OTHER AREA ATTRACTIONS: Kansas State Fair, Hutchison each September; the Kansas Cosmosphere and Space Center, 1100 N. Plum Street, Hutchinson, KS 67501, phone 620-662-2305.

EDITOR'S CHOICE: We recommend staying at the Sunflower Inn in Yoder and dining at the Carriage Crossing.

BRIEFLY

For a number of years Yoder was considered "The Amish Frontier", one of the farthest west Plain settlements.

HISTORY AND INDEPTH INFORMATION

There's still a frontier feel to this very traditional Amish community perched on the Kansas prairie. If you are looking for lots of shopping and endless all-you-can-eat buffets, keep looking. You won't find it here. But if you are looking for an authentic Amish experience, friendly folks, and tie in your visit to Yoder with a look around nearby Hutchinson, you'll have a wonderful weekend trip.

The signature event of the year in Yoder occurs the fourth Saturday of August when the village comes together to celebrate Heritage Day. Yoder Heritage Day is small festival where Amish and English mingle side by side and participate in good natured games and fun. It's a rare day of frivolity for a people not known for it. A typical Yoder Heritage Day includes a 6 a.m. Pancake and Sausage breakfast (locals call them "feeds"), horse plowing, and wheat thrashing demonstrations, buggy races, and draft horse pull. The event is capped off with fireworks in the evening.

Whenever you choose to come to Yoder stay at the Sunflower Inn. What makes this charming bed & breakfast unique is that it is in a former Amish home and buggy shop. One of our best night's sleep ever was while staying at this inn, snug in a comfy bed while listening to the constant Kansas wind whispering across the prairie. Start your day with one of innkeeper Kendra Horst's homemade coffeecakes. She herself has an Amish background and the recipe has been passed down.

The Carriage Crossing in Yoder offers family style dining and traditional American fare. Amish bakers tackle dessert with a mouth-watering selection of homemade pies. Carriage Crossing features a carry-out bakery so you can take a favorite pie with you. Flavors include traditional favorites like cherry and blueberry to offbeat, but decadent, pies like Snickers Bar and Chocolate Peanut Butter Cream Cheese.

Elsewhere in town, take a step back in time by visiting Yoder Hardware and Lumber, 9816 S. Main Street, Yoder, KS 67585, phone 620-465-2277, which bills itself as, "truly an old-time hardware store with horseshoes, hand tools, crocks, butter churns, hand meat grinders and sausage stuffers. We sell nails in the bulk, weighing each purchase on an old metal scale. We carry a full line of Radio Flyer metal wagons, tricycles, bicycles and toys, as well as their line of miniatures and collectibles."

Twenty five minutes west of Hutchinson is another Plain community. A Beachy Amish Mennonite church sprawls across the area as does an Amish settlement. The Amish settlement here is a bit more progressive than others. Seeing buggies on the road is actually uncommon (Sundays for church are when you'll see them most) here, instead you'll see monster-sized tractors being driven as the main mode of transportation. Automobiles are not permitted. A couple of places worth checking out in Partridge:

THE POTLUCK, 12109 W Illinois Ave, the Miller family (Beachy Amish Mennonite) operates a produce stand in season. Stop here for fresh veggies, eggs, and meats.

GLASS SPRINGS DAIRY, 5702 W. Longview Rd., Hutchinson KS 67501, phone: 620-669-8127. This is a family-run dairy at the Jacob Beachy Farm. They offer both fresh and frozen raw (unpasteurized) whole milk. Kansas is a state where selling and consuming raw milk is legal. In addition, they have eggs, grass fed beef, an assortment of canned jellies and vegetables that are available for purchase on their farm.

MAINE

New England's plain presence has been minimal over the years. The reasons are several. The first explanation is historical. Two hundred years ago most Amish first arrived in North America into the welcoming arms of William Penn's Pennsylvania. And back then the natural migration route was westward, not north, so Amish settlements sprung up in Ohio, Indiana, Illinois and Iowa, but rarely did people head north. Secondly, the tendency for Amish has been to seek out large rural tracts of land where they could live in agrarian isolation and populous New England has generally lacked that. Maine, however, has a more rural, rugged flavor than its other more crowded neighbors and that has proven to be a draw for the Amish in recent years.

While Maine does not have enough of an Amish population for us to devote a ton of space to in this book, we do think that "Plain Maine" is worth a look for New Englanders. The Amish communities in New England also seem more open to "seekers," a term used for outsiders who seek to join the Amish faith. And we think this Plain population will continue to increase in Maine as Amish find the ruggedly independent streak of the state and the cheap land prices attractive.

IMPORTANT AT-A-GLANCE INFORMATION

AFFILIATION: Old Order Amish, progressive

UNITY

This is a quiet, small settlement that started as a daughter community of the older and larger Smyrna church.

You'll want to first stop at the Community Market, 358 Thorndike Road. This is more a general store than the typical bulk food emporium favored in many Amish settlements. At the Community Market you can find anything from lawn furniture to bird feed to baked goods.

Another place you'll want to check out is the Living Grains Bakery and Locust Grove Woodworking at 256 Ward Hill Road, Thorndike, ME 04986, phone 207-948-9663. The Living Grains Bakery offers an array of products made from whole grains freshly ground on site. Katie Copp and her daughters bake three days a week using an old wood cook-stove. Their bakery is open on Fridays and Saturdays and their products are also sold at the Community Market on other days. Meanwhile, Kenneth Copp crafts custom handmade furniture pieces in his woodshop. Our favorite places to purchase Amish-made pieces are the small shops based at someone's home. Here you usually find the owners have a stake in their products and you can most often be assured that what you are purchasing is the Plain craftsmanship passed down from generation to generation.

If you are going to visit the Unity community, we found that staying in Bangor was a good bet. Bangor has all the major services of a big city and you can also squeeze in a visit to gorgeous Bar Harbor and nearby Acadia National Park.

Pssst!

Two items of note when visiting the Amish settlement in Unity: first, plan your visit for Wednesday morning. That is when fresh doughnuts are sold at the Community Market, 368 Thorndike Road, Unity, ME 04988. 207-948-4174 is their phone number, call ahead to verify.

Secondly, Unity is a rare Old Order community that has a formal church building. Inquire at the Community Market about Sunday service times. We think it's easier and less awkward to attend a service that is in a church building than someone's home.

SMYRNA

IMPORTANT AT-A-GLANCE INFORMATION

AFFILIATION: Old Order Amish, progressive

The Amish church in Smyrna is similar in philosophy and character as the Unity church. The Unity church is considered a "daughter church" of Smyrna. Key difference between this Old Order Amish church community and others is that instead of growing and spreading out to include multiple church districts, the churches here prefer to keep their size to one congregation. The congregations are to serve as "witnesses" or "beacons" to outsiders, beacons of spirituality, family, and faith. Once a church grows to the size of about 25 families, a small group will split off and start a settlement elsewhere. We predict Maine will be hopscotched with small, self-contained Amish communities within the next 20 years. The progressive, spiritual (but not overtly evangelical) bent of this church has drawn Amish from diverse areas (Kentucky, Tennessee, Ohio).

When visiting Smyrna's Amish community, two places you'll want to stop:

PIONEER PLACE GENERAL STORE, 2539 US Route 2, Smyrna, ME 04780, phone 207-757-8984. This Amish-owned store has become popular with locals for its wide selection of everything from jams, and breads to locally made furniture.

MERRI GOLD GREENHOUSE, 156 Currie Road, Smyrna, ME 04780. An Amish-owned greenhouse that sells all sorts of plants accustomed to the sometimes harsh Maine climate.

FORT FAIRFIELD

This is a new community in the far northern reaches of one of our farthest north states. Many of the Amish moved to this remote redoubt to get away from tourist traffic and suburban sprawl. A handful of Amish families live here scratching a living from the rocky Maine soil just miles from the Canadian border. There is one Amish business that we know of: Zook Family Farm, 266 Maple Grove Road, Fort Fairfield, ME 04742. In addition to offering fresh produce during season they also sell hand-made wooden chairs, swings, rocking horses, tables, and natural goats milk soap. Most of the wood furniture is Adirondack style and made from pine or spruce. If you have a chance to visit this community let us know what you think at **thewilliamsguide@gmail.com**

IMPORTANT AT-A-GLANCE INFORMATION

AFFILIATION: Old Order Amish, conservative

PLAIN MAINE: WHO ARE THE SHAKERS?

Sometimes people lump the Shakers in with the Amish. Like the Amish, Shakers have become well known for pacifism, simplicity, self-sufficiency, hearty scratch-made foods, and superb craftsmanship. So while they do share some sociological and anthropological traits, the religious roots of Shakerism are completely separate from the Amish. Shakers emerged from a utopian religious movement in the 1700s. But Maine is home to the only surviving Shaker community. Three Shakers hold out in the Sabbathday Lake Village, 707 Shaker Road, New Gloucester, ME 04260. Since Shakers can only join the church by conversion (celibacy is a defining trait of the church and perhaps an ill-advised one if a church is bent on growth) the movement never blossomed. Visitors are welcome to the Sabbathday Lake Village which was founded in 1793. Sabbathday Lake was always considered "out in the boonies" and was always the smallest Shaker colony, so there's some irony that it is the last one standing. As of 2013, three Shakers still lived and pracited the faith at Sabbathday Lake.

Visitors are welcome to explore the village grounds and visit the museum.

GETTING THERE

The Village is 25 miles north of Portland, and 12 miles west of Lewiston-Auburn.

From the south (Boston, Portland): Take Gray-Exit 63 off the Maine Turnpike. At the traffic light at the toll booth turn left to Route 26A. Go to the next set of traffic lights and bear right into Route 26A. Stay on Route 26A until it merges with Route 26 North. Follow Route 26 North for approximately eight miles to Shaker Village (watch for large black and white road signs).

From the North (Augusta, Bangor): Take Auburn Exit 75 off the Maine Turnpike. Turn right at the toll booth onto Routes 100, 4, 202. Follow that route for one mile and turn right onto Route 122. Follow Route 122 over hill and dale until you come to Route 26. Turn left onto Route 26 South. Follow Route 26 South for about 2 miles and you will be at the Shaker Village. The Village is about eight miles from Exit 12 (watch for road signs) on the Maine Turnpike.

Meals are not available at the Village. A wide selection of restaurants are located within 10 minutes of the Village in the towns of Gray, New Gloucester, Poland, and Auburn.

Some Shaker services are open to the public, call the Shaker Village at 207-926-4597 for more information.

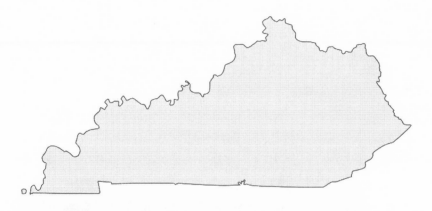

KENTUCKY

CROFTON

HIGHLIGHTS: Many people unfamiliar with the Amish (and even some who are) mistake this church for Mennonite because they do allow electricity and motorized tractors. It's one of the few horse and buggy Amish communities that we know of that permit limited electricity. The other is Partridge, Kansas (see page 94). What we like about the Crofton community is the rare chance to interact and enjoy a meal with the area Amish in a non-restaurant setting. The suppers are made by members of the Amish church and served in their own community building. The meals are served the first Friday of each month (they often take a summer hiatus). The meals begin at 5 p.m. and continue through 8 p.m. The menu is served buffet-style and usually includes barbecued pork and chicken (southern specialities), sweet creamed corn, mashed potatoes and plenty of homemade pie. The supper is $8 for adults, $4.50 for children, under 5 eat free. superb supper opportunity to to experience Amish culture first hand

IMPORTANT AT-A-GLANCE INFORMATION

AFFILIATION: New Order Amish, progressive

Directions to Crofton, KY

Take I-24 exit 86 and head towards towards Hopkinsville.Turn Right on Pennyrile Parkway. Exit at interchange 23 (Crofton) and then make a left when exiting hwy. Drive 2.5 miles and drive through tiny Crofton. You'll see the Amish community building on the right.

through food. There are usually some horse-drawn buggies in the parking lot and plenty of Amish attend the suppers and dine with non-Amish who attend. A wonderful chance to mix and learn!

The Crofton Consignment Auction is held each April at the community building. Call the community building 270 424-3090 for the exact date, but the auction features Amish-made crafts, farm implements, baked goods, and furniture.

Both the auction and the monthly suppers are used as fund-raisers for the local Amish schools and medical funds.

Another place we like in Crofton is Country Cupboard, 12040 Madisonville Road, Crofton, KY.

Phone: 270 424-8888. Over half of The Country Cupboard is mainly a dent/closeout grocery store. The other half of the store has a lunch meat and cheese area, where you can order sandwiches. They have a small bakery where fresh bread, pumpkin rolls, and fried pies are baked on Thursday and Fridays. There is also a large selection of baking items: cake and cookie sprinkles, chips, coconut, flours, sugars, dried fruits, etc. There is one aisle that has men's black hats, a few sewing threads, and housewares.

Pssst

WHAT IS AN AMISH COMMUNITY BUILDING?

Community buildings are becoming increasingly common in Amish settlements, but they are not without some controversy. In addition to the potlucks and plays, some Amish communities will use them for funeral visitations. The Amish have traditionally worshipped in their homes and traditionalists fear these buildings could be a first slide down the slippery slope towards abandoning that custom.

MICHIGAN

The Wolverine State's Amish presence is most dense on the Lower Penninsula. Michigan is more industrial than rural, so the Amish population has limited room to grow. The largest concentration is in the south near Sturgis and Centreville, with a growing community in Hillsdale County. There are also Amish churches in the Belding area and up the US 131 corridor through the west part of the state. Other sizable settlements can be found near Clare, Mio, and Marlette.

**IMPORTANT AT-A-GLANCE
INFORMATION**

AFFILIATION: Swartzentruber Amish

CLARE

As is typical of Swartzentruber Amish communities, there aren't a ton of tourist amenities here. But there are still ways one can explore and enjoy this settlement located in the center of Michigan's mitten.

Our favorite stop in this area is at 8441 East Surrey Road, the Jacob J. Miller produce stand. This is a tiny roadside stand on a desolate stretch of street. But unlike many other Amish roadside stands, this one sells an amazing array of items in their tiny roadside booth. In addition to the usual in-season produce, the Miller booth sells quart jars of home-canned, home-made pie filings. On past visits they've had cherry, strawberry-rhubarb, and peach. Also sold are home-canned relishes, crisp homemade pickles, and some baked goods. We've visited plenty of produce stands over the years in Amish country, but this one makes our top five list because of its simplicity, variety, and charm. This is a stand the size of a couple of phone booths (remember those?), but a lot of various delicious items are packed into this stand.

Clare is also a fun place to go for its Amish auctions which feature an authentic Amish experience and a chance to help local schools. The third Friday and Saturday in May and the final Friday and Saturday in August feature a quilt auction, craft show, and flea market on the grounds of Simon and Barbara Yoder's farm. This is a wonderful opportunity to experience an Amish farm first-hand and sample some great food. The address is 10885 North Leaton Road and the auction is from 8 a.m. to 5 p.m. The auctions have become so well-attended that many of the vendors set up are not Amish. However, there are plenty of hand-made Amish quilts and food tents staffed by Amish bakers who churn out doughnuts, pies, and baked goods for the throngs in attendance.

More laid back event takes place the second Saturday of July and this is probably our favorite in the Clare community. Come at 4:30 p.m. to Simon and Barbara Yoder's farm for an all you can eat chicken and fish dinner. Supper starts at 4:30 with an auction beginning at 6 p.m., selling anything from calves to quilts. All proceeds from this auction go directly to the Amish school fund.

ST. JOSEPH COUNTY

Over 1500 Amish call the settlements around Colon and Centreville home. This area is a nice Amish escape from the more heavily tourist visited areas of northern Indiana. The local tourism bureau bills the area as "River Country" for the St. Joseph waterway which winds through the county, bisecting it north to south.

The heaviest concentration of Amish in the county are along the following roads: State Route 66, Nottawa Road, Wasepi Road, and Truckenmiller Road. The River Country Tourism people actually have a driving tour of their Amish settlement online on a handy map, click **thewilliamsguide.com/links** and look for St. Joseph County. You can then arrange your visit in a more orderly fashion. Following, in more haphazard fashion, are some of our favorite Amish businesses in St. Joseph County, Michigan.

IMPORTANT AT-A-GLANCE INFORMATION

AFFILIATION: traditional and progressive

During apple season we like to visit Riverside Apple Orchard, an Amish owned business at 28749 Hackman Road, Sturgis, MI 49091, phone 269-659-1966. During apple season they also serve up homemade cider-pressed doughnuts. Call ahead to make sure the doughnuts are available, as they only make them on certain days.

The Spring Creek General Store is an Amish-run general store at 24763 Spring Creek Road, Mendon, MI 49072. As the name implies this store sells a bit of everything from furniture to flour.

Miller's Discount Store, 24029 Truckenmiller Road, Centreville, MI 49032, phone 269-467-4935 is an Amish-owned store that also offers a wide range of goods under the gentle hiss of their gaslights.

Another favorite is Countryside Greenhouse at 25920 Wasepi Road, Centreville, MI, phone 269-467-4967. This Amish-run greenhouse applies their emerald thumbs to everything from spring vegetable plants to mums.

Plan your visit to St. Joseph County during the summer and your visit will be magical. The FAB Magic Manufacturing Company, 212 East State Street, Colon, MI 49040, phone 269-432-4017, is headquartered here and each summer they host a four day magic festival. The 2014 schedule has it from July 23 – 26 and is billed as a time when magicians from all over the world gather to display their talents and share knowledge with other fellow magicians, amateur and professional.

The Amish are not doing a disappearing act in St. Joseph County. The community is Michigan's largest and oldest and has been experiencing a growth spurt lately with more Amish businesses opening.

BECOME A ROAD SCHOLAR

We have not enrolled in this program, but we wanted to make our readers aware of this option. The Amigo Centre, 26455 Banker Street Road, Sturgis, MI 49091, phone 269-651-2811, (a Mennonite retreat) has teamed up with the Road Scholar program, phone 800-454-5768, to offer a unique Amish immersion experience. The five day program costs $669 and includes meals in an Amish home, study of their culinary culture, noodle making, and immersion. The program promises a traditional "Thrasher's Meal" in an Amish home (a huge harvest feast) and the chance to meet and talk to Amish shopkeepers and people in the community. Overnights are at the Amigo Centre. The program also promises a chance to:

Pssst!

There is a restaurant in St. Joseph County that bills itself as Amish. We have not been to this establishment before and don't know much about it. Please give us any reviews at **thewilliamsguide@ gmail.com** and we'll update in future editions and online. The restaurant is called The Amish Table at 701 E. Main Street, Centreville, MI 49032, phone 269-467-4181.

• Learn how the Amish lead their daily lives during field trips through this beautiful farmland region.

• Visit with a young Amish couple who operate their own Amish store, specializing in herbs and natural health remedies.

• Meet the proprietors of Amish shops featuring quilts, dry goods, baked goods, and furniture.

Again, we have no experience with this program, but it sounds like the type of one-on-one cultural immersion opportunity that we really enjoy. We also like the fact that the program is coordinated through the Mennonite-operated Amigo Centre. The Roads Scholar program is a life-long learning, non-profit organization that has been offering adult courses since 1975.

MISSOURI

The Show-Me-State has had a slow increase in Amish population over the years. We've often been perplexed by the state's relatively small Amish community because it would seem to be ideal: plenty of rural, reasonably priced farmland, centrally located to the Midwest, and a temperate climate. The largest Amish community in the state is a Swiss Amish settlement near Seymour and the larger, more traditional community near Jamesport. The Amish population elsewhere does seem to be growing.

BOWLING GREEN

Bowling Green is a Swiss Amish settlement with roots in the Berne-Geneva area of Indiana. This means that customs, traditions, and language follow a slightly different trajectory (see page 10). The last name Schwartz is very common here which immediately identifies the area as being of Swiss origin.

IMPORTANT AT-A-GLANCE INFORMATION

AFFILIATION: Swiss Amish

This Amish settlement is small and off the beaten path, but it does feature a dozen or so businesses open to the public. It is a conservative Amish community and some businesses like Hickory Stick Woodworking or Kemp's Woodworking and Furniture specifically requests tourists not stop in to meander, only serious buyers.

Its proximity to St. Louis (about 90 miles northwest) and heavily traveled I-70 makes this an ideal afternoon getaway.

Most of Bowling Green's Amish businesses are located south and southwest of the town. One interesting place to note is Jacob Schwartz General Store and Buggy Shop. With only about 75 Amish families in the area there's not enough business to do buggies only, so owner Jacob Schwartz also runs a general store at the same location.

You can find a wonderful map of Bowling Green's Amish community at **www.thewillliamsguide.com.**

CLARK

This is a settlement that we would like to explore more, so watch future editions of The Williams Guide for updates and information. We've been to this community before, but not enough to include an indepth entry in this edition. Clark's Amish settlement is an easy hop off I-70 for those traveling and want to experience a low-key, non-touristy Amish community. Most of the Amish businesses are located in the countryside northeast of the village of Clark. The Clark Amish community is rapidly growing, counting some 9 church districts in the area.

Some favorite stops of ours in Clark include:

South Side Sales, 866 Audrain Road 110: This Amish-owned bazaar sells over 150 types of spices and an array of fresh produce that attracts customers from all over. They also specialize in hand-made cedar lawn furniture.

IMPORTANT AT-A-GLANCE INFORMATION

AFFILIATION: Old Order Amish, conservative

Bontrager's Bakery, 2882 Audrain Road 175: This business is a two for one. Marie Bontrager runs a bakery, while her husband Ora runs a leather and harness shop. Check out an array of wonderful baked goods here which include homemade sourdough bread and oatmeal bars.

Clark Produce Auction, 1966 Hwy Y: All auctions begin at 10:30 a.m. with produce sold by the box, bin, or cart. We are told another highlight of this auction is the Amish-made homemade ice cream, rich and creamy and always on hand.

Stay tuned to future editions of The Williams Guide for updates on Clark.

JAMESPORT

PROVISIONS: Jamesport Grocery, 102 South Broadway, Jamesport, MO 64648, phone 660-684-6616, is an old-time small-town sundry store offering everything you might need for a day of picnic and exploring Amish country. For those staying in Chillicothe, there is a full-service Hy-Vee Supermarket at 1210 Washington Street, Chillicothe, MO, phone 660-646-3638.

DINING: There aren't any authentic Amish restaurants in Jamesport, per se. But there are what we call Amish-style restaurants. Gingerich's Dutch Pantry, 118 Broadway, Jamesport, MO 64648, phone 660-684-6212, and the Country Cupboard, 1011 W Old Highway 6, Jamesport, MO 64648, phone 660-684-6597, offer hearty country fare.

GETTING THERE: From Kansas City take Interstate 35 to Missouri State Route 6 east and follow to Jamesport.

OTHER ATTRACTIONS: Just an hour to the east of Jamesport, try to rekindle the magic that ignited

IMPORTANT AT-A-GLANCE INFORMATION

AFFILIATION: Old Order Amish, traditional

LODGING: There are a couple of chain motels in Chillicothe, which is about 20 minutes from Jamesport. If you want to stay closer to the Amish community, we recommend the Arbor Country Inn, 103 Olive Street, Jamesport, MO 64648, phone 660-684-6760, an oasis of amenities in a pretty rural area. For more information, visit **http://www. jamesport.net/arbor/**

the career of one Walt Disney. The famous inventor, imaginer, and Mouseketeer grew up in this tiny Missouri town. You can visit the Walt Disney Hometown Museum, 120 E. Santa Fe Avenue, Marceline, MO 64658, phone 660-376-3343, for a fascinating look at the early life of this giant of American pop culture.

BRIEFLY

With eight sprawling church districts, the Amish settlement outside of Jamesport is one of the largest communities west of the Mississippi.

HISTORY AND INDEPTH INFORMATION

The first Amish began settling here in the 1950s, attracted by cheaper land and more lenient rules on formal education. The settlement has grown over the years and now claims close to 180 families. There is also a population of German Baptist Brethren nearby. The German Baptists dress plainly, but they do drive cars and have electricity (see page 10)

Keep in mind when planning a visit to Jamesport that most Amish businesses are closed on Thursdays. Also, in our "hyper-connected" world it's easy to forget that there are still some rural places where cell phone service is non-existent. Many areas outside Jamesport have little to no cell phone service as of this edition's publication.

Jamesport has evolved into a community with a lot of commerce. Yet it is also a very traditional settlement without overbearing tourist traffic. So if you are seeking a pleasant escape and chance to immerse yourself in Amish culture, Jamesport would be at the top of anyone's list.

Some places you'll want to check out include the cluster of stores which some jokingly call "The Amish Mall." H & M Country Store, Countryside Bakery, and the Fabric Barn are all clustered right together.

COUNTRYSIDE BAKERY, 21870 State Highway 190, Jamesport, MO 64648, phone 660-684-6720, sells a heavenly assortment of freshly baked bread, noodles, dinner rolls, wide variety of cookies (including such Amish classics as Monster Cookies and Snickerdoodles) and a mouth-watering selection of pies.

H & M COUNTRY STORE, 21910 State Highway 190, Jamesport, MO 64648, phone 660-684-6848. Lavern and Sue Beechy run this amazing bulk food emporium that offers everything from homemade peanut fudge to 50 pound bags of whole wheat flour. This is a typical staples store that you find in most Amish settlements and this one is definitely a destination if you come to the Jamesport settlement. The Beechy's make H & M a "sampler store", putting out free samples of various items to munch on as you browse.

FABRIC BARN is located next door to H & M Country Store. Sells bolts of material and sewing supplies.

You can't just go to one Amish bakery. You'll have nothing to compare and contrast! So your next stop should be Anna's Bake Shop, 1005 Old Hwy 6, tucked away quaintly in a non-descript white house. Each morning the smell of hot homemade glazed doughnuts lifts into the air. Anna's hours are 8 a.m. to 6 p.m., but get there early if you want one of the fresh doughnuts. They go fast especially during peak tourist season.

GRABER GREENHOUSE & PRODUCE, 30707 State Highway 6, Jamesport, MO 64648, phone 660-684-6518, is a gardener's paradise, offering everything from color-filled hanging baskets to farm-fresh produce. In the autumn, Graber's turns into an apple wonderland with crisp, cold freshly-pressed apple cider for sale.

HOMESTEAD CREAMERY, 2059 LIV 506, Jamesport, MO 64648, phone 660-684-6970, this should definitely be on anyone's list of stops when planning a trip to Jamesport. The Homestead Creamery is run by the Flory family, who are German Baptists. They specialize in hand-made, home-made cheeses, especially Farmstead and Raw Milk cheese. The Flory's raise Jersey cows which supply plenty of milk for the fromage. Cheese samples are available daily, but if you can plan your visit for Tuesday morning that is when the public is invited on a cheese-making tour.

OAKRIDGE FURNITURE, 779 SW 80th Street, Jamesport, MO 64648, phone 660-684-6121,   offers a selection of Amish-made furniture, including roll top desks, bedroom suites, shelves, and wooden toys. This is an authentic Amish furniture shop run by Joe and Ada Burkholder, which is why we like the place. A family-friendly bonus: each Saturday, Oakridge offers "horse-churned ice cream" for sale. We're not sure how appetizing most people would say "horse-churned" sounds, but children of all ages are enthralled by one of the Amish buggy horses attached to an ice cream churn contraption.

JAMESPORT HARNESS, 21776 State Hwy 190, Jamesport, MO 64648, phone 660-684-6775, is a typical Amish harness shop. It's fascinating to watch the timeless art of harness making and as long as you're respectful of the proprietor's time, most welcome visitors to come in and look around and watch the work.

Dining options around Jamesport are limited, but there are a couple of places where people can indulge in Amish-style food. Probably the best example is Gingerich's Dutch Pantry in downtown Jamesport, 118 S. Broadway Street, phone 660-684-6212, which offers supper specialties like baked pit ham and roast turkey.

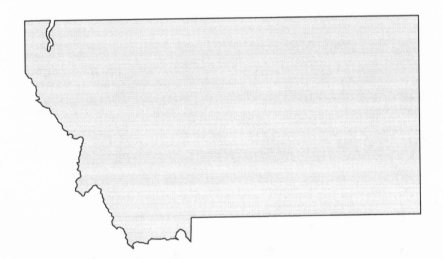

MONTANA

It all started in 1974 when the first Amish settled in Rexford, Montana. The community in Rexford has captured the Amish imagination for a generation. The Rexford settlement is perched almost on the Canadian border in the state's far, far northwest corner. More recently communities have sprung up in St. Ignatius, Gold Creek, and a couple of other places. At this writing, the state has five Amish settlements, but we expect the number to grow in the years ahead.

REXFORD, MONTANA

IMPORTANT AT-A-GLANCE INFORMATION

AFFILIATION: Old Order Amish, traditional

LODGING: Riverstone Family Lodge, 6370 US Highway 93N, Eureka, MT 59917, phone 866-345-0026, offers quaint cabins with views of the stark Montana countryside. Most cabins are duplexes so if you happen to stay during a crowded time you might be stuck with a noisy neighbor. A handful of other motels can be found around the town of Eureka.

PROVISIONS: Stein Family Foods, 33 Kaylin Lane, Eureka, MT 59917, phone 406-297-3151, is a traditional full-line supermarket. The deli will make sandwiches if you're planning a day trip into the mountains.

OTHER: Plan to bring your passport if you like to nose around, the Riverstone Family Lodge is only about 2 miles from the Canadian border.

FOOD: Café Jax, 207 Dewey Avenue, Eureka, MT 59917, phone 406-297-9084, is an eclectic mix of Old West and more progressive cuisine. There's even a veggie sandwich on the menu which is a real find in a state that offers sparse options for the meatless crowd.   Yong's Teriyaki Take-Out, 602 Dewey Avenue, Eureka, MT 59917, phone 406-297-7077, offers a wide selection of traditional Asian specialties. Visit the Koocanusa Café, 172 Gateway St Rexford, (406) 297-7997 for some delicious huckleberry shakes in season.

GETTING THERE: From Eureka, MT: take Hwy 37 West, 14 miles to Koocanusa Bridge, go west across the bridge, turn right (north) and follow the signs.

From Libby, MT: go north on Hwy 37, 52 miles to The Koocanusa Bridge, go west across the bridge, turn right (north) and follow the signs.

OTHER ATTRACTIONS: 3 ½ hours to the south and east (a short jaunt by Big Sky standards) is the awe-inspiring scenery of Glacier National Park. Explore the West Kootenai Amish community and then plan to explore Glacier National Park.

EDITOR'S CHOICE: Stay at the Riverstone Lodge, enjoy the ambiance of Eureka and a meal at Café Jax and then spend a Saturday in Rexford visiting the Kootenai Craft store, partaking in the buffet, and then plan on visiting Glacier National Park on Sunday when the Amish stores are closed.

BRIEFLY

Rexford is one of the most remote Amish settlements in the United States. But those willing to go out of their way will be rewarded with an authentic, rustic experience free from the traditional trappings of tourism. Yes, this is a long way from Lancaster!

HISTORY AND INDEPTH INFORMATION

Just getting to the Rexford settlement is an exercise in patience. It's a long way from anywhere. Rexford itself is just a mailing address. The actual Amish settlement is about 20 minutes away, a drive across the picturesque Koocanusa Bridge with a stark warning that you're entering "Grizzly Habitat". A parking area can be found at each end of the bridge and there is ample room on the bridge for pedestrians. A stroll onto the bridge to admire the deep blue waters of Lake Koocanusa is a must.

The Rexford settlement started in the early 1970s by a group of Amish men from east who were seeking a more outdoor oriented life. The ample fishing and hunting opportunities of Montana proved to be an irresistible lure. A large tract of ranchland being offered for sale proved to be a perfect fit and fast-forward four decades later the Amish settlement is still holding its own. Many young Amish men from out East continue to be drawn to the area's ample outdoor opportunities. There's a joke in Rexford that single Amish women from the East who are having trouble finding a mate should move to Rexford. The ratio of available men is usually far higher than that of women. Moose steaks, elk meat, and bear burger are all staples found on Amish menus here.

The Rexford community enjoys almost mythical status among the Amish. The community has been around for generations, its hearty inhabitants penning cookbooks and sharing tales with family out east about grizzly bears and moose. Yet we were surprised when we finally made it to Rexford at how small the settlement actually is. The population is often transient. People move to Rexford and after a couple of years the isolation proves too much. "For sale" signs are common.

Don't expect to see a ton of buggy traffic while visiting the West Kootenai Amish community. While buggies are seen on the roads occasionally, most Amish here use bicycles for traveling. The "hub" of the settlement is the Kootenai Store & Craft, 7217 West Kootenai Road, Rexford, MT 59930, phone 406-889-3588, an Amish-owned and operated sundry store. The hours of this store can vary, so before planning a trip it is best to call ahead. Saturday mornings feature an all you can eat buffet from 9 a.m. to 11 a.m. The meal features a fusion of classic western food and traditional Amish cooking. Seating for the buffet is limited, but call-ahead reservations are accepted. This is a rare opportunity for a home-cooked Amish-made meal, so come hungry!

The signature event of the West Kootenai Amish settlement is the annual school benefit auction held the second Saturday of each June. The auction features a smorgasbord of goodies from a huge selection of authentic hand-made Amish quilts, farm equipment, log homes, gazebos, and hand-made cedar furniture. A lunch, prepared by the local Amish community, is served usually featuring fried chicken, plenty of side dishes, ice cream, pies, and a variety of baked goods. As the name of the event implies, funds raised from the auction go to operate the community's schoolhouse.

On the way there or back be sure to stop in to The Koocanusa Café, 172 Gateway Street, Rexford, MT 59930, phone 406-297-7997, in the actual village of Rexford (not much more than a post office, general store, and campground). During the area's prized huckleberry season the Café serves homemade huckleberry shakes.

ST. IGNATIUS

IMPORTANT AT-A-GLANCE INFORMATION

AFFILIATION: New Order Amish

LODGING: The Sunset Motel, 32670 US Highway 93, St. Ignatius, MT 59865, phone 406-745-3900, offers no-frills, bare-bones accommodations for those on a budget. The motel is situated within 10 minutes of the St. Ignatius Amish settlement. People who want more upscale, but still affordable accommodations, should check out the Best Western KwaTaqNuk Resort, 49708 US Highway 93, Polson, MT 59860, phone 406-883-3636. The resort is about 30 minutes from the Amish settlement.

PROVISIONS: The Mission General Store, 61307 Watson Road, St. Ignatius, MT 59865, phone 406-745-7200, is an Amish-owned market on the edge of town. They sell most anything one would need. Try Rod's Harvest Store, 116 N. Main Street, St. Ignatius, MT 59865, phone 406-745-4275, for camera batteries, accessories, etc.

OTHER: You are on Tribal territory so obey all posted signage and respect Native American traditions and customs.

FOOD: The Old Timer Café, 278 Mountain View Road, St. Ignatius, MT 59865, phone 406-745-3240, offers a wide selection of traditional American favorites and breakfast all day. This diner is not Amish-owned but you'll see Amish customers frequenting this busy eatery. Be sure to stop by The Malt Shop, 101 1st Avenue, St. Ignatius, MT 59865, phone 406-745-3501, for huckleberry ice cream when it is in season. For a more traditional Plain dining experience visit The

Ronan Café, 113 Main Street SW, Ronan, MT 59864, phone 406-676-5404, about 20 minutes north of St. Ignatius. This Mennonite-owned restaurant offers an amazing array of homemade pies, scratch-made breads, and hearty entrees. Even the salad dressings are made from scratch.

GETTING THERE: From U.S. Highway 93, turn onto Main Street, take a left on Airport Road and another left on Foothill Road.

OTHER ATTRACTIONS: 20 minutes outside St. Ignatius is the National Bison Refuge in Dixon, MT 59831, one of the oldest havens for bison in the USA. The refuge is administered by the US Fish & Wildlife Service and today, 350-500 bison call this refuge home. Today, the National Bison Range is a diverse ecosystem of grasslands, Douglas fir and ponderosa pine forests, riparian areas, and ponds. The Range is one of the last intact publicly-owned intermountain native grasslands in the U.S. In addition to herds of bison, it supports populations of Rocky Mountain elk, mule deer, white-tailed deer, pronghorn, and bighorn sheep as well as coyotes, mountain lions, bears, bobcat, and over 200 species of birds. A visitor center provides context and history, but the highlight is a driving tour. The road that goes up into the mountains (Red Sleep Mountain Drive) is closed from mid-October through mid-May (the lower portion of the road remains open all year - called the Prairie Drive/West Loop).

EDITOR'S CHOICE: For dining we recommend the Ronan Café in Ronan, offering a wonderful array of Mennonite made pies, entrees, and salads.

BRIEFLY

The St. Ignatius settlement is the only Amish community located on Native American tribal lands. The Flathead Indian Reservation is home to the Bitterroot Salish, Kootenai, and Pend d'Oreilles tribes, sometimes known as the Confederated Salish and Kootenai Tribes of the Flathead Nation.

HISTORY AND INDEPTH INFORMATION

The Amish first started settling here in the 1990s. Under various Homestead Acts promulgated by the US government some tribal lands fell into non-Native hands over the years and were subsequently sold to Amish settlers. The tribe is trying to buy back all land from non-Natives. Don't expect to see the Amish selling fry bread anytime soon or interacting too much with the Native American population. The growing Amish presence at the base of the Mission Mountains around St. Ignatius has ignited some friction between long-held Native traditions and the more individualistic Amish. But attempts have been made recently to mend fences.

The Amish settlement is located several miles east of St. Ignatius at the base of the towering Mission Mountains. A "must stop" for anyone visiting this Amish community is the Amish-owned Mission General Store. The store offers a full line of groceries and Amish goods. On one of the days we visited there was an Amish woman sitting outside the store selling delicious homemade cinnamon rolls.

Drive the rural roads on the valley floor and explore. You may even see an old-fashioned cattle drive in progress and some of the young cowboys are Amish teenagers helping out.

Two of our favorite stops in the St. Ignatius community are:

MISSION GENERAL STORE, 61307 Watson Rd, 406-745-7200 This is a great starting point for your visit to the St. Ignatius Amish settlement. This store is in many ways a typical Amish-owned bulk food store of the kind that are so common out east. But with few mainstream grocery options in the area, Mission has become a bustling hub. When we visited once on a Saturday morning an Amish woman was selling homemade cinnamon rolls out front, so in addition to bulk foods, you may get lucky and score some baked goods.

MONTANA BIRD & GARDEN, 32040 Allison Road, 406-745-5115: This business is owned by Ed Beachy, originally from Holmes County, Ohio where he still owns and operates the Berlin Seed catalog. Stop in to the small retail store here to satisfy any seed needs or wild bird supplies. The store is located on the beautifully landscaped grounds of Ed and Brenda Beachy's home.

The signature event of the year is the annual auction that raises proceeds for the Amish Christian School. The auction is usually held the Saturday after July 4th. Come early for an all-day auction featuring quilts, pre-fabricated cabins, gazebos, sheds, and yard furniture. The auction also features an amazing array of hand-made quilts. All items sold are Amish made. And if you don't come for the auction, come for the barbecued chicken lunch, homemade pies, and other baked goodies sold. The Amish school is located at the corner of Allison Road & Foothills Road.

Explore the back roads and enjoy some of the many gorgeous gardens of bright wildflowers that the Amish cultivate in their yards. Keep an eye out for buggies, but also bicycles as they are a common and convenient mode of transportation on the flat valley floor.

Many Amish enjoy visiting the nearby National Bison Range where an incredible driving tour is open to the public. Hear the bugling of elk and spot bobcat, bear, and bison in this federally protected wilderness, one of the oldest refuges for bison in the USA. Stop in to the interpretative center first to learn about the refuge's history.

A visit to the Flathead Native American Museum, 708 Main Street, Polson, MT 59860, phone 406-883-3049, adds context to the area's heritage.

The Other Plain in Big Sky: Hutterites

Montana is home to a number of Hutterite colonies, a group closely related to the Amish and Mennonites historically and culturally. The main difference between the groups is that the Hutterites live communally on colonies while the Amish and Mennonites do not. The communal nature of Hutterite life limits cultural exchange, but you can find Hutterite-raised meat and produce at Farmer's Markets in Montana. The plain dressing Hutterites are often mistaken for Amish or Mennonites. Hutterite colonies are found in the Canadian prairie provinces and through Montana,the Dakotas, and Minnesota in the United States. They embrace cutting-edge technology for their generally agrarian operations.

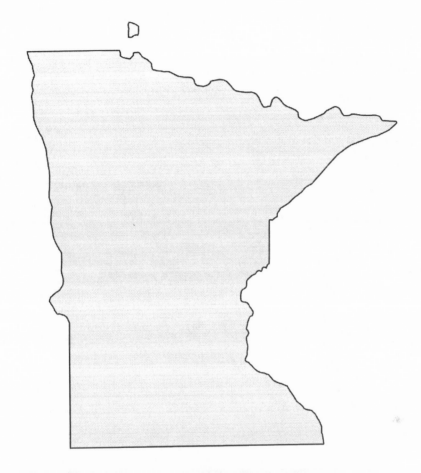

MINNESOTA

MINNESOTA

HARMONY

IMPORTANT AT-A-GLANCE INFORMATION

AFFILIATION: Swartzentruber Amish

LODGING: There are chain motels and hotels in Rochester, about 45 minutes away. Or for a bit more rustic accommodations try the Amish Country B & B, 13086 County Road 23, Canton, MN 55922, phone 507-421-8429.

PROVISIONS: An old-fashioned IGA in the heart of Harmony offers a full line of groceries and picnic supplies for your visit. The IGA is located at 55 Center Street West, Harmony, MN 55939, phone 507-886-2225.

FOOD: To our knowledge, no Amish restaurants in the area.

GETTING THERE: The community of Harmony is located on US 52, one

HARMONY

of the longest pre-interstate highways in the country, going from North Dakota to Charleston, South Carolina. From the north, take exit 218 off of Interstate 90 in Rochester. Follow US 52 south for approximately 45 miles until you reach Harmony. From the south, take US 52 from Decorah, Iowa about 30 miles to Harmony.

OTHER AREA ATTRACTIONS:

BRIEFLY

The Harmony community is Minnesota's oldest and largest settlement nestled among the rolling hills of what is known as the "Bluff Country".

HISTORY AND INDEPTH INFORMATION

Like the Amish in Ethridge, Tennessee (see page 202) this is a sprawling Swartzentruber Amish community. This isn't someplace you probably would want to plan a whole vacation around but for people in the Upper

Midwest interested in the Amish, this is a settlement that is best enjoyed by just exploring the back-roads looking for those ubiquitous hand-lettered signs selling everything from homemade honey to snickerdoodle cookies. The Amish communities around St. Charles, Preston, Canton, and Harmony are growing and we hope to explore them more and include updates and an expanded entry in future Williams Guide editions. Meanwhile,this is one of the more accessible Amish businesses in the area that you'll want to check out!

ROADSIDE STAND, 12668 US Highway 52, Canton/Harmony. This is exactly what the name suggests, a road-side stand. The road side stand is open April through October and offers everything from locally grown produce to homemade egg noodles, pies, bars, cookies, cakes, and crafts. The stand is run by Joseph and Amanda Hershberger.

MINNESOTA NICE: The Amish population in this cold, northern state has been steadily increasing. The more temperate southeastern part of the state has seen the biggest growth, but Amish communities are now seen as far north as Wilmar and a settlementment in the far, far northwest near Fergus Falls. Might neighboring North Dakota be the next frontier for the Amish?

MISSISSIPPI

The Magnolia State has had a minimal Plain presence over the years, but recently their proximity to Tennessee has made the northern part of the state attractive to Amish who have outgrown the Ethridge community.

PONTOTOC

IMPORTANT AT-A-GLANCE INFORMATION

AFFILIATION: Swartzentruber Amish

The Amish settlement is located just to the southwest of the town of Pontotoc. Take highway 9 west out of Pontotoc, head south on Route 341 and then right onto Salmon Road. Travel 5 miles and you're in the heart of the settlement, you can also follow signs where about a dozen Amish homes offer goods for sale from their home-based businesses, from baskets to breads.

What we find interesting about this community is the infusion of southern-meets-Amish cuisine, homemade foods that you can't find in any other Amish settlement. This corner of northeast Mississippi is about the northernmost range where peanuts can be successfully grown on a large scale and this Amish settlement has embraced this earthy food that made Jimmy Carter successful before entering politics. Some families in this settlement sell homemade peanut brittle year-round along with scratch-made peanut butter syrup. Thick and peanutty, it's the perfect pancake topper. Other southern specialties sold from homes in the area include muscadine jellies and fresh muscadines, a type of wild grape regional to this area.

Other items one can find in this settlement are homemade baskets and baked goods, like cinnamon rolls. Not sure that we'd recommend planning a vacation around Pontotoc but if you're in the area anyway, this is a superb opportunity to interact with some of the most conservative Amish in a very no-frills, non-touristy setting.

NEW YORK

No state has seen its Amish community grow faster over the past 10 years than The Empire State. Far from the glittering lights of the Big Apple, buggies are now clattering down rural areas of the Mohawk Valley, within sight of the shore of Lake Ontario, and throughout the rural "North Country" on the edge of the storied Adirondacks. For most of the 1900s and early 2000s the state's Amish community was centered around the quiet corner of the state where the sleepy city of Jamestown snores. And that is the area we'll focus on for this book, but we expect future revisions and updates to include more stops in New York State!

Conewango Valley-Jamestown, New York

IMPORTANT AT-A-GLANCE INFORMATION

AFFILIATION: Old Order Amish, conservative

LODGING: Jamestown offers plenty of chain motel lodging and there is the Cherry Creek Inn, see "Editor's Choice" below.

PROVISIONS: Wegman's has a store in Jamestown at 945 Fairmount Avenue, Jamestown, NY 14701, phone 716-483-9900. This regional grocery store has a cult following and is a perfect place for picnic supplies and anything else you might need from sushi to sandwiches. Closer to Cherry Creek, there is South Dayton Supermarket, 1 Pine Street, South Dayton, NY 14138, phone 716-988-3410, a classic throwback of small-town grocery charm.

FOOD: The Cherry Creek Sub, 6775 Main Street, Cherry Creek, NY 14723, phone 716-296-8103, this shop offers basics such as pizza and subs. There are plenty of eating establishments in Jamestown.

GETTING THERE: To Jamestown: From the west, take I-86 E to exit 12 for NY-60 toward Jamestown. From the north, take I-90 W to exit 59 for NY-60 toward Dunkirk/Fredonia, then take NY-60 S. From the east, take NY-17 W/Southern Tier Expressway to exit 12 for NY-60 toward Jamestown. And from the south, take I-79 N to exit 178A to merge onto I-90 E toward Buffalo, then take exit 37 to merge onto I-86 E toward Jamestown, then take exit 12 for NY-60 toward Jamestown.

OTHER ATTRACTIONS: Jamestown's favorite daughter is celebrated annually at the Lucy Comedy Fest and the Lucy Desi Museum, 10 West 3rd Street, Jamestown, NY 14701, phone 716-484-0800. The legendary comedienne was born in Jamestown and spent much of her childhood here.

EDITOR'S CHOICE: We recommend staying at the Cherry Creek Inn, 1022 W Road, Cherry Creek, NY 14723, phone 716-296-5105. The inn, centrally located to the area's Amish country, provides a serene escape from the hustle and bustle of city life and provides a seamless stay in the quietude of Amish country. The inn bills itself as a "sanctuary for all seasons" and we concur. The inn includes a library, a hot tub and all the country charm of a century-old inn.

BRIEFLY

New York State has one of the fastest growing Amish populations in the USA as of 2013. The largest growth is occurring in the Mohawk Valley of Central New York and in an area known as The North Country. But long before those areas began attracting legions of Amish, the Jamestown area was the state's "Plain hub." Amish starting moving to the area in the 1940s and as of this writing comprises 24 sprawling church districts.

HISTORY AND INDEPTH INFORMATION

The toughest decision you'll have to make when visiting western New York's Amish country is where to stay. And this depends on your personal preference. If you've never stayed at a bed & breakfast before, you might want to make the Cherry Creek Inn your first. If you prefer the anonymity and amenities of a chain motel, there are plenty of places to stay in Jamestown. Jamestown is a perfectly pleasant place to use as a base to explore this area's rich Amish culture. We find the proprietor Sharon Howe-Sweeting to be the perfect innkeeper. If you want to be left alone, she'll leave you alone. If you want someone to chat up about your world travels and have friendly conversation, she's equally good at that. Innkeeper aside, the sprawling Victorian home built in 1864 is reason enough to stay. The home is living, breathing history. Breakfast pastries are baked by a local Amish woman and you can dine in the breakfast nook and watch buggies clip-clop past.

If you are seeking a no-frills Amish experience, without a ton of the tourist trappings offered in other areas, the Conewango Valley is a place you want to consider visiting. There are plenty of unique and different Amish-owned home-based businesses to keep you busy from ironworks to quilts to toys. Quaint hand-lettered signs point the way to most places.

We were lucky enough to be in this area during sugaring season when homemade maple syrup was on the menu. The Amish in the area sweeten their cereals with syrup, add the tasty treat as a flavoring to baked goods and just make a general way of life with their sugaring in the late winter and early spring. When the sap rises so do the spirits of many of the Conewango Valley Amish.

Many of the Amish-owned businesses in the area don't have names, just signs pointing the way to "fresh eggs", "homemade maple syrup", or "hand-made toys." A visit to the Conewango Valley becomes a bit like a treasure hunt. As you explore the back roads you'll make your own discoveries depending on the season and what home-based business you're lucky enough to stumble upon. And then you can crash in the evening at the Cherry Creek Inn. We highly recommend this trip and inn.

MALINDA'S CANDY SHOP, 12656 Youngs Road, Conewango Valley, NY 14726: Visit here close to Easter and you'll be treated to an amazing array of chocolate bunnies and eggs. But Malinda's creations don't stop with just chocolate. You'll find homemade and other fun edibles. We bought two pieces of candy that looked just like deviled eggs. She used white chocolate for the "egg" part and some yolky colored candy for the center. It was too creative to eat!

MILLER'S BAKERY, 12624 Seager Hill Rd (Rt. 62), Conewango Valley, NY: This must-stop destination offers a mouth-watering selection of fruit-filled pies, their crusts glowing golden, plump loaves of homemade bread, and maple-glazed doughnuts that would make the sweetest tooth surrender.

RABER'S TOYS, 11363 Pope Road, Randolph, NY 14772: We love this store, because it is like a veritable trip to Santa's workshop of yesteryear. You won't find video game consoles or any other battery-powered wizardry here. What you will find is a lot of wooden toys, games, and imagination-driven fun. Dan Raber is the Old Order Amish proprietor and he'll custom make items or make his own from horse-shaped swings to shelves.

OHIO

We are unsure why Ohio has become the Plain Capital of the World, or at least a close second to Pennsylvania. Pennsylvania we can understand. It's where the Amish first settled in the USA and home and history are difficult to divorce. But, Ohio? It's a largely industrial state with Cincinnati, Columbus, and Cleveland sprawled out across the state in a diagonal sash. The only answer we can come up with is that it is close to Pennsylvania. For all of Ohio's industrial hubs and suburban sprawl there are surprisingly large swaths of rural, agrarian areas that the Amish find attractive. For years Holmes and Geauga County were the cradles of Amish country in the Buckeye State, but now there are Amish communities in virtually every corner. We expect that Ohio's Plain population will continue to grow, but that eventually the population will become too dense and more and more Amish will move westward.

OHIO

DARKE COUNTY

DARKE COUNTY DAY TRIP:

THE "OTHER" HORSE AND BUGGY PEOPLE

People are generally familiar with the Amish and Mennonites with their horse-drawn buggies and simple ways. But a lesser known Plain group living primarily in parts of California, Kansas, Indiana, and Ohio also dress plainly and some even travel by horse-drawn buggy.

Western Ohio is home to the largest concentration of German Baptists in the world. The Amish and Mennonites capture most of the media fascination and public interest. But the German Baptist brand of plainness has many of the same appeals as the Amish: an adherence to simplicity, a rich faith, strong families, and diversity within the faith. On one end are the Old Order German Baptist Brethren who still use horse and buggies and on the other are much more progressive New

Conference German Baptists who use computers, cars, and the internet but still dress plainly.

Exploring the rural roads of Darke County can be like a step back into time. Here our some of our favorite Brethren businesses in the area.

THE FLOUR BARREL, 8136 US Route 36 West, Bradford, Ohio 45308, phone 937-447-4925. This is an Old Order German Baptist Brethren owned bulk food store that offers a little bit of everything from bulk foods, deli meats, cheese, noodles, Christian books, and canning supplies.

COUNTRY CLOCK SHOP, 7804 Childrens Home-Bradford Road, Bradford, OH 45308, phone 937-448-2533. This is an amazing old-time clock shop.

JULIA'S CONFECTION CONNECTION, 111 Marvin Street, Gettysburg, OH. This is a tiny store tucked into a garage with limited hours (Tuesday, 11 – 7; Wednesday – Friday, 11-5:30, and Saturday, 9 – 12), but there is an incredible assortment of baking supplies from pans to sprinkles. Also custom made cakes that celebrate the rich tradition of Brethren baking. And if you're lucky you'll stop in on a day when some of the store's hand-made caramel-wrapped, chocolate-dipped pretzels are in stock. Yum!

KINGS POULTRY FARM, 8091 Horatio-Harris Creek Road, Bradford, OH 45308, phone 937-448-2448. Stop here for all sorts of fresh farm goodies. Antibiotic, hormone-free and humanely raised poultry is the speciality.

Visitors are welcome to attend Brethren services and we recommend doing so if you're genuinely interested in Plain culture. The services are a bit more accessible than Old Order Amish ones, yet a lot of the same values of faith and family are equally emphasized.

OTHER: If you're going to be in the area anyway, might as well visit the grave site of "Little Miss Sure Shot", Old West legend Annie Oakley who is buried near here. She is buried in Brock Cemetery. The site of the graves of Annie Oakley and her husband Frank Butler, are located on Beamsville-St. Marys Road, just off U.S. 127 near Ohio 185. Each July the county seat, Greenville, hosts the Annie Oakley Festival to honor their favorite daughter.

HARDIN COUNTY/ BELLE CENTER

FOOD: There are plenty of Mom & Pop restaurants in Kenton, but no Amish restaurants in the area for meals.

GETTING THERE: US 68 provides a convenient artery from the north or the south. Hardin County is located about 45 minutes due east of I-75.

EDITOR'S CHOICE: We recommend Mary Slabaugh's Bakery on 12813 County Road 265, north of Pfeiffer Station, Kenton, Ohio 43326. Mary is Old Order Amish and her bakery turns out a wonderful array of mouth-watering treats from homemade doughnuts and coffeecakes to cookies and pastries. We also recommend the Tinker Toy Shop on County Road 146.

IMPORTANT AT-A-GLANCE INFORMATION

AFFILIATIONS: Old Order Amish (conservative), Degraff, Ohio; New Order Amish, Belle Center; Old Order Amish (traditional), Hardin County

LODGING: There is a chain hotel in the county seat, Kenton. A little farther from the Amish areas, you might try the Inn at Ohio Northern University, 401 West College Avenue, Ada, OH 45810, phone 419-772-2500. Ada is a quintessential college town and offers a cosmopolitan contrast to the under-the-radar Amish.

PROVISIONS: Fresh Encounter, 2021 Broad Avenue, Findlay, OH 45840, phone 419-422-4826, is a local grocery store near Kenton that offers a full line of essentials.

BRIEFLY

This often overlooked Amish community thrives an hour north of metropolitan Dayton, the birthplace of aviation.

HISTORY AND INDEPTH INFORMATION

Why visit Hardin County when the largest Amish settlement in the world beckons just 90 minutes to the east? The answer can be found in the question. Because being the largest brings with it belching tour buses, bumper to bumper traffic, and can bring crowded restaurants. If that isn't your cup of tea and you're simply seeking a no-frills Amish experience, look no farther than this quaint county.

What truly sets Hardin County apart from other Amish communities in Ohio are the broad range of home-based businesses. This is a place where you can spend a day just meeting and visiting with Amish people. Stop by the Hardin County Chamber of Commerce at 225 South Detroit Street, Kenton, Ohio 43326, phone 419-673-4131, and pick up a brochure about the area's Amish community. On the brochure there is a very handy map that respectfully lists dozens of Amish businesses from toy stores to greenhouses. You can also visit **thewilliamsguide.com** and print out the brochure. The brochure is your gateway to a day of wonderful shopping and visiting among the Old Order Amish.

Two businesses we do recommend highly are **MARY SLABAUGH'S BAKERY** on 12813 County Road 265, Kenton, Ohio which offers an array of mouth-watering pastries, cakes, and cookies. Doughnuts and colorful Jello cookies are specialties. Make this one of your first stops because the best stuff often sells first. Pies are especially quick to disappear.

THE TINKER TOY SHOP on County Route 146 is a father and son furniture and toy store. No electronic playthings or video games here, just hand-made wooden toys that stimulate the mind and decorate a child's room, plus amazing handcrafted furniture from beds to vanities. While some "Amish furniture" stores reek of assembly-line big box stuff, this store is the real deal. They will custom-make anything a customer asks.

The rest of your day (or days, you could easily spend 2 days here) can be spent carefully cruising the back roads buying anything from local honey to fresh flowers to eggs and zucchini.

CHRISHOLM: AN OLD OLD ORDER COMMUNITY

Visitors flock to Amish settlements across the USA and Canada to get a taste of the simpler life to contrast with today's harried and hurried pace. But what were the Amish like 150 years ago? A remnant of an early Amish community still survives among the hubbub of Cincinnati's northern suburbs and local historians are doing their best to preserve it for future generations.

Amish settlers first came to the banks of the Great Miami River some 30 miles north of Cincinnati because they were attracted by the fertile farmland and rural isolation. Christian Augspurger was the bishop presiding over 300 Amish families who would eventually call Butler County, Ohio home. Throughout the 1800s the community thrived. Christian Augspurger built a stone farmhouse with outbuildings and christened it Chrisholm. After his death in 1848 the farmstead passed to his son Samuel. By the early 1900s the church membership had dwindled due to ideological and theological divisions. Some congregants moved to Illinois and Iowa while the rest remained, eventually establishing a Mennonite church in nearby Trenton which survives to this day.

1n 1989 the 258 acre Augspurger farm with house, an 1890's Pennsylvania style barn, outbuildings, and family cemetery was taken over by a non-profit group called Friends of Chrisholm. Today visitors can tour the farmstead every day from 8 a.m. to dusk. The farmstead is now part of the Butler County Metroparks system. For more information about Chrisholm, visit **Chrisholmhistoricfarmstead.org**. The site's address is 2070 Woodsdale Road, Trenton, OH 45067.

ADAMS COUNTY

PROVISIONS: A Kroger grocery store, 210 Sterling Run Blvd., Mt. Orab, OH 45154, phone 937-444-6910, in nearby Mount Orab offers a full selection of provisions.

FOOD: The Murphin Ridge Inn offers elegant dining using locally sourced and seasonal produce. Keim Family Market, 2621 Burnt Cabin Road, Seaman, Ohio 45679, phone 937-386-9995, an Amish-owned bakery, offers made-to-order sandwiches and a huge selection of snacks, and baked goods. Blake's Soda Shoppe, 206 North Market Street, West Union, OH 45693, phone 937-544-2451, offers an old-time soda fountain experience and TJ's Railroad Restaurant, 19261 State Route 136, Winchester, OH 45697, phone 937-695-9009, offers traditional American diner fare.

GETTING THERE:

From Cincinnati: take Ohio 32 east about 40 miles.

IMPORTANT AT-A-GLANCE INFORMATION

AFFILIATION: Old Order Amish, traditional

LODGING: Several places offer a range of options for travelers. A Budget Host Inn, 18760 Ohio 136, Winchester, OH 45697, phone 937-695-0381, caters to the budget-minded and a Comfort Inn, 55 Stern Drive, Seaman, OH 45679, phone 937-386-2511, for those who prefer a more traditional hotel experience. The Murphin Ridge Inn, 750 Murphin Ridge Road, West Union, OH 45693, phone 937-544-2263, (see editor's choice below) offers outstanding bed & breakfast/country inn accommodations.

From Parkersburg, West Virginia: Take US 50 west to Athens, then follow Ohio State Route 32 80 miles.

From Columbus: US 23 south to Ohio 32 west.

OTHER AREA ATTRACTIONS: Serpent Mound State Memorial is a 348-foot-long, three-foot-high prehistoric effigy mound located on a plateau of the Serpent Mound crater along Ohio Brush Creek in Adams County, Ohio. A creaky viewing tower allows visitors to see the entire earthworks from above. The park entrance is at 3850 State Route 73. Visit the Edge of Appalachia Preserve at 3223 Waggoner Riffle Road, West Union, Ohio. The park offers one of the most biologically rich ecosystems showcasing a variety of trails, flora, and fauna in this unique region where the western edge of the Appalachian meets the flatlands of Ohio.

EDITOR'S CHOICE: Hands-down favorite: Murphin Ridge Inn. Stay in the inn or one of their private cabins. For baked goods and sandwiches in the Wheat Ridge community, we recommend the Keim Family Market.

BRIEFLY

Adams County is home to what can best be described as Ohio's "other Amish Country." The community is tucked away in the rolling hardscrabble hills that some people refer to as "The Little Smokies", a picturesque bow to the much taller mountains by the same name in Tennessee.

HISTORY AND INDEPTH INFORMATION

The first buggies started clattering down the winding roads of Adams County in the early 1970s. Amish farmers were first attracted to the area by some of the cheapest land prices in Ohio. The community grew from its agrarian roots to include furniture production, tourism, and other home-based businesses. The community is known as the "Wheat Ridge" settlement, named after one of the many rocky ridges that crisscross the county.

We highly recommend using the Murphin Ridge Inn as your base to explore the area. The Inn is not Amish-owned, but it is centrally located within the Wheat Ridge community. From there you'll be able to easily visit Miller's Bakery, bulk food, and furniture stores. Their mouth-melting meals often include locally sourced vegetables and meats, some of which do come from Amish farmers. You can stay in either the main inn or one of the more private cabins on the grounds. Trails snake through the surrounding woods offering a peaceful view of the surrounding hills.

There are several signature events in this Amish community. One of our favorite and perhaps most unique is the Annual Amish Bird Symposium, billed as a day-long celebration of birds. The event began in 2003, held in the basement of an Amish home with a handful of bird enthusiasts in attendance and some speakers. A decade later the event has twice outgrown its venue and is now held in the Wheat Ridge Community building and attracts hundreds of attendees and some of the top-flight speakers in the avian world. Past speakers have included NPR commentator and writer, Julie Zickefoose and Kenn Kaufman, author of the guides that bear his name. Seating is limited so reserve your spot early at adamscountytravel.org. Even if you only have a passing interest in birds, the event is worth attending just for the Amish made lunch (vegetarian and non-vegetarian options) and homemade doughnuts by Amish baker, Clara Yoder.

Another sure bet is the Wheat Ridge Herb Festival held for three days each October (visit www.wheatridgeherbfestivals.com for exact dates). The festival is held each year on the Grindstone Farm, a non-Amish farm in the heart of the Wheat Ridge community. This celebration of everything herbal includes vendors offering herbal and medicinal teas, soaps and lotions, herbal rubs, blends, and butters. The timing of the festival usually coincides with the peak leafing season, exploding the rugged hills with hues of orange, purple, and brown.

The Wheat Ridge settlement continues to add more activities for visitors with a 5K run and half marathon being sponsored by Miller's Bakery and Furniture the final Saturday of September. Miller tells us, "The Adams County "The Adams County Half Marathon is a 5k run on September 28, 2013 at 8:00 am. It begins at Miller's in West Union, Ohio east of Cincinnati. All participants completing the run will be awarded a unique Amish finisher medal. All participants receive a tee shirt and goody bag. The course will go by four Amish schools in the area where Amish children will hand out water to runners. Registration is online at Tristateracer.com. Packets may be picked up at Miller's Bakery & Furniture, 960 Wheat Ridge Road in West Union, OH 45693." Call 606-831-3260 for more information.

The timing of the event is also in the midst of Amish harvest season when the seasons change from summer to autumn and Ohio prepares for this most festive period with fairs and festivals galore. The Wheat

Ridge Amish homestead of the Miller family is nestled in southern Ohio Appalachia country.

Our favorite past-time in Adams County, regardless of the time of year, is to explore the tiny ribbons of road that unspool across the hills. You'll take a trek back into time as you pass Amish harness shops and one-room schools (there are three in the Wheat Ridge community). And be sure to drive across the historic Harshaville covered bridge. The Harshaville Bridge, over Cherry Fork on County Road C-01-E (Wheat Ridge Road), was one of very few bridges not destroyed as Morgan's Raiders marauders blazed through the area during the Civil War. The 557 mile-long John Hunt Morgan Heritage Trail of Ohio winds over the bridge and through Adams County with some of the trail's 56 interpretive signs posted. Exploring the back roads, especially during spring, summer, and autumn allows the visitor to discover a variety of home-based businesses: Amish families selling fresh eggs, produce, wild bird supplies, and occasionally, baked goods. Colorful wash flutters on laundry lines and bountiful vegetable gardens are the norm. In season you'll often see Amish produce vendors selling fresh vegetables at the corner of Ohio 32 and Route 41. Be extra alert for slow-moving horse-drawn vehicles which can appear seemingly out of nowhere in the deep hills, twists, and valleys of Adams County.

Other must-stop spots are the following Amish-owned businesses:

KEIM FAMILY MARKET: We remember when this bakery was started in the 1980s by Roy Keim from the back of his buggy on Ohio 32. The Keim's grew their business over the years so that it is now a one-stop emporium offering furniture, bulk foods, and baked goods. Homemade crème horns and warm, soft, puffy pretzels are favorites. 2621 Burnt Cabin Rd, Seaman, OH 45679. Open six days a week, call ahead 937-386-9995

Pssst!

We'll let you in on a little "secret" about The Home Place. The Home Place is run by Delbert and Susan Schlabach who have roots in northern Indiana's Amish settlement. Susan learned how to make peanut butter pie at the knee of Amanda Yoder, creator of the legendary peanut butter pie found at Yoder's Restaurant in Pinecraft, Florida (see page 25). So the peanut butter pie sold at The Home Place is essentially a twin of the one found at Yoder's and it doesn't disappoint with a creamy, silky, peanutty filling topped with a light meringue on top. So anyone in southwest Ohio who doesn't want to travel to Florida for peanut butter pie need look no farther than The Home Place!

MILLER'S BULK FOODS, FURNITURE, AND BAKERY: An amazing array of furniture and food, Miller's a must-stop for any visitor to Adams County. Miller's is located at 960 Wheat Ridge Road, West Union, OH 45693. Miller's sells some of the most mouth-watering kettle corn we've ever tasted in generous-sized bags overstuffed with the sweet and salty confection.

THE HOME PLACE: This is a Mennonite-owned business and it is not even in Adams County, but it is a quick 10 minute journey east on State Route 125 to US 68. The address is 7771 US Route 68, Georgetown, OH 45121, phone 937-378-3400. This is the final stop on the "Crème Horn Trail." Both Keim, Miller's, and The Home Place are all legendary for their home-made crème horns, each with a slightly different filling. So you'll have to try all three! The Home Place also offers a selection of Amish-made furniture,a deli, and bakery. The Home Place is known for their homemade granola. Susan made some at first and experimented with selling it. People began coming back in and looking for more. They'd all come in asking "Hey, where's the granola?" So Delbert realized that they needed to keep making it.

LIFE'S A BEACHY

The Home Place (see above) is a store owned by a Plain family near Georgetown, Ohio. This community is not Old Order Amish, but neither are they Mennonites. They are known formally as Beachy Amish Mennonites. The Beachy group split from the Amish in 1927 in Somerset, Pennsylvania. It's been described to us that the Beachy Amish are a little more progressive than the most "liberal" Amish.   The Beachy Amish share much in common with the Old Order Amish but unlike the Amish they have meetinghouses for church, Sunday School, and a Bible School for young adults. The biggest difference is probably use of the automobile, which separates them from horse-and-buggy groups. Beachy Amish groups a can be found in many states but this is a far smaller group than the Amish.

OHIO

HILLSBORO-SINKING SPRING-BAINBRIDGE, OHIO

IMPORTANT AT-A-GLANCE INFORMATION

AFFILIATIONS: Old Order Amish (traditional), Swartzentruber Amish, Old Order Mennonite

LODGING: A couple of chain motels can be found in Hillsboro.

PROVISIONS: A Super K-Mart, 1249 North High Street, Hillsboro, OH 45133, phone 937-393-8323 (not to be confused with the smaller, more commonly found Big-K) offers a full line of groceries, camping supplies, and provisions. Super K-Marts were an experiment to compete with Wal-Mart and Target stores that sell full lines of groceries, the concept never really caught on, but it remains in Hillsboro.

FOOD: We recommend saving your appetite for your stops in Bainbridge (see below).

GETTING THERE: From Cincinnati, take US 50 to Hillsboro. From the north take I-71 to US 35 to US 62 south in Washington Court House.

OTHER ATTRACTIONS: After a day spent exploring the area Amish and Mennonite communities we recommend capping your visit off with a visit to Chillicothe to see Tecumseh. The outdoor drama runs from June 7 - August 31, 2013. (Monday - Saturday) Backstage Tours depart at 4:00 PM and 5:00 PM daily, Monday - Saturday, Adults $4.50 and Children (10 and younger) $3.50; visit the free Prehistoric Indian Mini Museum; dine in the open-air Terrace Restaurant; and visit the Mountain Gallery Gift Shop before experiencing one of the nation's finest outdoor productions.

EDITOR'S CHOICE: Dutch Kitchen, 4417 State Route 41 South, Bainbridge, OH, phone 740-634-2710, for breakfast. JR's General Store, 4715 State Route 41 South, Bainbridge, OH, phone 740-634-2194, for lunch. Country Crust Bakery, 4918 State Route 41 South, Bainbridge, OH, phone 740-702-7677, for afternoon snack, and Dutch Kitchen again for supper. For hand-made baskets, Stutzman's Basket Shop at 11976 Sinking Spring Road, Sinking Spring, Ohio.

BRIEFLY

A few years ago this location never would have merited a mention in this book. The first Amish didn't arrive in Highland County, Ohio until 2006. But now there is a thriving, diverse Plain community in a swath from Hillsboro to western Ross County and northern western Pike County.

HISTORY AND INDEPTH INFORMATION

This area does not have a long history with the Amish. With other Amish settlements becoming crowded and congested, some Amish families began scouting elsewhere in Ohio rural Highland County where the land was plentiful and the prices cheap. Miles from the nearest interstate, the insular isolation was appealing and the first Amish families began arriving after the year 2000. Now numerous Amish church districts can be found, from the most conservative to more progressive.

SINKING SPRING, OHIO: We recommend the Stutzman Basket Shop at 11976 Sinking Spring Road. Hours may vary and you can't call ahead, so try to stop by during "business hours" on a weekday or Saturday. The Stutzman's have dozens of homemade baskets packed into their free-standing shop, all crafted carefully by member of the family. Each basket has the name and age of the Stutzman family member who made the basket penciled on the bottom. The store also features some homemade candles and crafts by oldest daughter Amanda Stutzman. And if you really get lucky you might happen in on a day when Mattie Stutzman has some fresh jams or jellies for sale in the store.

The Old Order Mennonites

By Kevin Williams, Editor

I had heard glowing reviews of an "Amish bakery" along route 41 in the far northwestern corner of Pike County, Ohio. I was unfamiliar with the Amish in this area so one chilly winter's day I set out for this seeming no-man's land. Soon I found myself in a small vinyl-sided bakery with big plate glass windows in front and back. Busy bakers churned out some of the best confections I've ever tasted (and that is saying something!). I had to find the owner.

"He's back at the house, would you like to talk to him?" one of the kapp-clad workers asked, pausing to wipe flour from her hands onto her apron.

"Oh, yes, definitely," I said, mesmerized by the sweet smells in this bakery heaven.

Snowflakes were swirling outside and I was eyeing the thin sheen of ice accumulating on the highway out front, but I was on a mission. Luke Martin met me at the door, a tall, lanky man. I admired his willpower. If I owned that bakery, I'd be much more portly. I introduced myself and he graciously invited me inside where we sat at his kitchen table.

"So people kept telling me great things about this "Amish bakery" in Bainbridge, so I had to come see for myself."

"Well, first, let's get one thing straight. We're Mennonites."

And thus began a crash course on the differences between Mennonite and Amish culture.

The Old Order Amish and Old Order Mennonites share many similarities theologically and sociologically.

SIMILARITIES:

- Use of horse and buggy

- Generally speak a dialect of Pennsylvania Dutch

- Generally shun use of "on the grid" technologies like TV, electricity, and internet

DIFFERENCES:

- Old Order Mennonite men are clean-shaven, whereas Old Order Amish men grow beards

- Old Order Mennonites worship in a church building (called a meetinghouse) whereas the Amish generally hold services in private homes

COUNTRY CRUST BAKERY, 4918 State Route 41 South, Bainbridge, OH: This is one of our favorite "Amish" bakeries in the country. Except, it's not Amish, it's Old Order Mennonite. We like how the entire bakery is so open and and airy and inviting. You can watch the confections being made. We vote their whoopie pies the "best of the best", especially the peanut butter. Two giant peanut butter cookies smooshed together with a rich layer of peanut butter filling in between. Amazing! You can't go wrong with much at Country Crust, whether it's their coffeecakes, fry pies, breads, rolls, or pies. They also offer a savory selection like made-to-order sandwiches on a pretzel bun, homemade pretzels, and pizzas. Grab one of the picnic tables outside and enjoy your lunch or snack as the old-time tableau of southern Ohio's Mennonite settlement moves before you.

JR'S GENERAL STORE, 4715 State Route 41 South, Bainbridge, OH: We love this sprawling bulk food store. First, it's amazing how gas lights and skylights can make a person forget about electricity. Secondly, they have an amazing deli offering up a wide selection of made-to-order sandwiches. Fill out a slip of paper on the counter where you specify your sandwich specifications and then watch it be custom-made or browse elsewhere and wait for your number to be called. JR's has a massive selection of bulk foods, from soup bases to spices to trail mix. Anyone who cooks or bakes from scratch will find this store a must-stop. Another part of the store features handcrafted furniture and Mennonite-made quilts. They have an entire aisle dedicated to batteries and various kinds of fuel-burning lamps, so don't forget to pick up an extra hurricane lamp or two, if you are running low. We recommend bringing your cooler to this out of the way store so you can load up on cheeses and other items that might need to be put on ice.

CRAFTS UNLIMITED/DUTCH KITCHEN: 4417 State Route 41 South, Bainbridge, OH, this restaurant is run by Old Order Mennonites, one of the few dining options anywhere that is actually owned and operated by Plain people. The menu is simple but hearty. Come hungry and prepared to browse the crafts.

BAINBRIDGE PRODUCE AUCTION: The Bainbridge Wholesale Produce Auction is located in the heart of the Bainbridge Old Order Mennonite settlement about five miles south of the Village of Bainbridge on 14211 Barrett Mill Road, Bainbridge, OH 45612, phone 937-365-1263. Sales begin in April and run through the growing season, typically ending in early November. Most of the items are sold to retailers, but there are small lots available for individual buyers. It's fun to just visit the auction and linger to watch the wheeling and dealing, listen to the candent call of the auctioneer, and watching buggies pulling and in and out of the parking lot with their produce.

GEAUGA COUNTY

IMPORTANT AT-A-GLANCE INFORMATION

AFFILIATION: Old Order Amish (traditional)

IMPORTANT AT-A-GLANCE INFORMATION

ACCOMODATIONS: There are plenty of chain motels in nearby Willoughby and Ashtabula. While we can't personally vouch for The Red Maple Inn, this quaint bed and breakfast has been a reader favorite. Contact: 14707 S Cheshire Street, Burton, OH 44021, phone 440-834-8334, or visit redmapleinn.com.

PROVISIONS: We really like Giant Eagle, a regional grocery store chain located at 15400 West High Street, Middlefield, Ohio. Stock up on picnic supplies or camera cards here.

FOOD: There are several dining options in Geauga County that allow one to experience Amish culinary culture. Mary Yoder's Kitchen is a popular draw for people who are passing through. See full entry below.

GETTING THERE: From Columbus or Cleveland, take Ohio State Route 87 east from Interstate 271.

We first became acquainted with the Geauga County Amish community over 20 years ago. Since that time the settlement has grown to become what some consider to be the fourth largest in the world. As Cleveland's eastern suburbs have spread, the Amish in Geauga County often find themselves pressed up against suburban sprawl. But we do have some favorite places to visit. If you go to Geauga County, leave home with an empty refrigerator because there are an amazing variety of organic produce and homemade goodies which you might want to bring home.

Geauga County lacks some of the natural scenic beauty of other Ohio Amish enclaves (Holmes or Adams County, for instance) but it makes up for it by offering a very authentic Amish experience: few kitschy tourist stops and plenty of home-based businesses to peruse.

Here is a sampler of some of our favorites:

MILLER'S ORGANIC PRODUCE, 17201 Bundysburg Road, Middlefield, OH: Additional products are available at the farm: free-range eggs, honey, maple syrup, Miller's Country jams, and produce (in season).

D & S FARM SALES, 4738 Gates Road East, Mesopotamia, OH: This an organic farm run by Daniel Fisher and sons (hence the D & S). For city slickers wanting to see a working farm, this is a great place. Some of the items available at the farm include a wide variety of produce, as well as turkeys, chickens, ducks, geese, and eggs. Bread may be available on Fridays and Saturdays. In addition to vegetable farming, the Fisher family runs a farm and garden supply store. The store supplies minerals and supplements for farmers' fields, as well as for farmers' families.

HERSHBERGER'S HOUSEWARES, 15419 Madison Road, Middlefield, OH, phone 440-632-9065: The name of the store makes one think of pots and pans or maybe some appliances, but the reality is that the store is so much more. The front section is a bookstore, stocking many Christian titles and Amish books. The main part of the store features Amish clothing of all sorts (most Amish make their own clothing, but buying some is nice in a pinch).

AMISH HOME CRAFT SHOP AND BAKERY, 16860 Kinsman Road, Middlefield, OH, phone 440-632-1888: This is a quaint, cozy shop that offers a variety of items including handmade quilted items including bed quilts, placemats, table runners, and more. Amish-made baskets are plentiful as well as handmade Amish wood products (toys, puzzles, shelves, and more). A selection of Amish clothing is offered along with shelves of locally made Amish jams and jellies and pickled veggies. A couple of tables are stocked with homemade, hand-made baked goods including breads, pies, cookies, fried pies, and more.

MEL'S SHOES N MORE, 16189 Burton Windsor Road, Middlefield, OH, phone 440-636-5815: We love this Amish-owned store because it is a throwback to the days before big box stores stomped out the Main Street Mom and Pop shoe proprietors that populated so many Main Streets. In addition to shoes and work boots, Mel stocks scarves, socks, and other accessories.

ERB'S VARIETY STORE, 13924 Bundysburg Road, Middlefield, OH, phone 440-632-0376: This emporium of everything offers bulk foods and groceries, canning supplies, stoves and stove parts, kitchenware, toys, gift items, as well as meats and cheeses. Ask about their discount for items bought by the case. Their hours are Monday through Friday 8:00 am until 5:00 pm and Saturday from 8:00 am until 4:00 pm.

S & E COUNTRY STORE, 17574 Newcomb Road, Middlefield, OH, phone 440-632-9999: Here you will find German and English books, gifts, toys, and oil stove parts. They also offer oil stove repair.

Speaking of stoves, this next business maybe a bit of a snore to some, but we are trying to focus on Amish-owned businesses in this book whenever possible and JMJ Enterprises fits that bill. Run by Amish entrepreneur James Miller and his wife, this is the place to go if you are searching for fireplace products. JMJ is located at 15848 Nauvoo Road, Middlefield, OH, phone 440-632-0780, and specializes in stoves, fireplaces, and inserts for Amish and non-Amish alike, servicing all of Ohio.

B & K SALVAGE is located at 5515 Kinsman Road, Middlefield, OH, phone 440-632-1538. B & K is part of a growing trend in Amish settlements, affectionately known as "bent and dent" stores. Amish entrepreneurs cull expired, slightly damaged, or overstocked goods so you can get anything from great deals on laundry detergent, diapers, or cookies. Hours are Monday through Wednesday 8:00 am until 5:00 pm, Thursday and Friday 8:00 am until 6:00 pm and Saturday 8:00 am until 3 pm.

SUGAR VALLEY MAPLE: The Amish of Geauga County take advantage of the area's lush sugar maple groves to create lip-smacking syrup each spring. During sap season stop by this Amish-owned sugar bush. James Miller runs an 1,800 tap pipeline at 15771 Chipmunk Lane (south of SR 87 between White Road and Lake Street), Middlefield, OH 44062, phone 440-785-0005.

MARY YODER'S AMISH KITCHEN, 14743 Old State Road, Middlefield, OH 44062, phone 440-632-1939: This is a convenient place to go for an Amish-style meal. We have not sampled this place yet, so we can't offer a first-hand assessment, but this restaurant appears to be typical of other Amish-style restaurants offering up a hearty buffet, great portions, and convenience. Visit MaryYodersAmishKitchen.com for more information and if any of our readers have dined here, please email us your experiences at **thewilliamsguide@gmail.com.**

We have two recommendations for in-home dining in Geauga County.

RACHEL YODER: The first Friday of the month means that Rachel Yoder clears her living room to serve dinner by reservation. Up to 50 people can dine on a Friday evening supper. Rachel Yoder serves a mouth-watering fried, then baked chicken, seven layer salad, rolls, mashed potatoes and gravy, and vegetables. Her creamed peas have earned legions of followers. For dessert there is date pudding and three kinds of pie. For information or to make a reservation, call the Yoders at 440-834-0406.

EMMA'S HOME COOKING: Mike and Emma Slaubaugh also open up their home for meals by appointment only. The theme of the supper is an Amish wedding meal and the menu consists of: fruit cup, seven layer salad, baked chicken, mashed potatoes and gravy, stuffing, green beans, homemade bread and jelly, date nut pudding, and choices between lemon meringue, apple crumb or cherry pie. The minimum size group they serve is 12, so gather a group of friends or you may be able to "piggyback" onto another group. For more information call the Slaubaughs at 440-693-4617.

Pssst!

We are big believers in using food to explore culture. Scratch cooking and hearty meals are as much a part of Amish life as buggies and home-based church services. If you are willing to make some schedule adjustments and do some sleuthing, there are home meals to be had in Geauga County's Amish community. At these home meals, you'll experience genuine Amish ambiance in an Amish home along with good company and the comfort food that is part of the culture.

TO TOUR OR EXPLORE?

Tour buses are as much a part of the landscape of large Amish settlements as buggies, barns, and windmills. The tours are clearly popular or there wouldn't be such a high demand for them and the buses would be out of business.

Whether you take an organized tour of Amish country or go solo is purely an issue of personal preference. We at The Williams Guide prefer to explore solo than to go on a tour. We think the advantage of being able to explore at your pace and on your own schedule outweighs the more regimented experience of a formal tour. Some of our favorite moments in Amish country over the years have been unplanned, spontaneous moments that probably wouldn't have happened had we been on a scheduled tour. That having been said, we visit Amish country all the time. If you are limited on time and access to Amish country and you want to make sure you "hit all the right stops", then a tour could be for you. Also, if you are someone who just isn't a fan of driving, then why not let someone else do it for you? Tour bus drivers will be experienced in sharing the roads with slow-moving buggies.

If you are interested in an organized tour, many of them include the option of a meal in an Amish home. This alone is worth the price of admission in our opinion. Just do your homework before selecting a tour partner. Here are a couple of tour guides in various areas that we can recommend.

EDITOR'S CHOICE! AMISH HEARTLAND TOURS: Proprietor Lavonne Debois does a super job of providing a holistic experience in Holmes County's Amish country. Many of Heartland's tour guides have an Amish or Mennonite background. Contact

Amishheartlandtours.com or by phone at Amish Heartland Tours at 330-893-3248. If you are going to take a tour, we recommend Amish Heartland.

OHIO AMISH TOURS: This group focuses more on the Geauga County Amish settlement and a standard package does include a meal in an Amish home, which we highly recommend. For more information visit ohioamishtours.com or call 440-693-4000.

AMISH TOURS OF HARMONY, Minnesota: Since this is such a conservative Amish community, it can be difficult for an outsider to make inroads. And since this is a much smaller settlement than, say Holmes County, Ohio, the tours are more up-close and personal. Most of the tours are in private car or van. For more information visit amish-tours.com or call 507-886-2303.

Of course there are tours in almost any sizable Amish settlement but these are just a sampling of the ones we are familiar with. Check future guides for updates and additions.

OHIO

IMPORTANT AT-A-GLANCE INFORMATION

AFFILIATIONS: Old Order, New Order, Swartzentruber, Beachy Amish, Old Order Mennonite

THE AMISH ARCHIPELAGO:

Holmes, Wayne, Tuscarawas and surronding counties.
GETTING THERE:

From Cleveland or Akron, Ohio:
Take Interstate 77 south to exit 83 (Dover/Sugarcreek) and go west on State Route 39 through Sugarcreek to Berlin. See map and Getting There from Berlin below.

From Pittsburgh, Pennsylvania:
Take 22 west to Cadiz, Ohio. At Cadiz, take State Route 250 west to Interstate 77. Take Interstate 77 north to exit 83 (Dover/Sugarcreek) and go west on State Route 39 through Sugarcreek to Berlin. See map and Getting There from Berlin below.

From Columbus Ohio: From Columbus take Interstate 270 east to 161 to 62 to Gahanna. Proceed north on State Route 62 to Millersburg. Head east on State Routes 62/39.

Ohio has the largest concentration of Plain people in the world. Trying to pin down exactly where the borders are of the settlement is tough because church communities are constantly shifting and spreading. So we're calling the region the "Amish Archipelago" because it's generally one large area bordered by Navarre in the north and Gambier-Walhonding in the south. To the northwest the Amish area extends beyond I-71 to the Ashland-Nova area and southeast to Dundee, although more and more Amish are now moving towards Carrollton and Cadiz so the southeastern boundary is shifting.

For over 60 miles from Gambier in the south to Navarre in the north, and from Nova in the Northwest to Dundee in the southeast.

The Amish Archipelago can be explored in a day or a week depending on your preferences.

EDITOR'S CHOICE For more upscale accommodations we recommend the Inn at Honey Run, 6920 County Road 203, Millersburg, OH 44654, phone 330-674-0011. For more budget-minded travelers we recommend Zinck's Lodging on the Square, 4703 State Route 39, Millersburg, OH 44654, phone 330-893-6600.

BRIEFLY

Holmes County is the largest island in the Amish Archipelago and by the year 2020 will become the majority Amish county in the USA!

HISTORY AND INDEPTH INFORMATION

The Amish first began coming to Holmes County in 1809, attracted by the area's isolation and arable farmland. Sociologists estimate the population of Holmes County – fueled by Amish families that often have 8, 9, and 10 children - doubles each generation. So while it took generations for the Amish population to become noticeably large, now Holmes County is largely Amish.

What is the best way to see this largest Amish community in the world? This all depends on your schedule. Someone who asks us this question and only has a couple of hours to spend in the area will get a different answer than someone who has a couple of days. To the "drive-byers" we say the single best way to experience Amish country is to take State Route 39 into Holmes County and then just explore capillary-like network of lanes that wind their way across the hills. While many rural areas have a criss-cross grid to explore, Holmes County roads are like spools of grey thread that randomly unwind across the hills. Get off the main road and explore and you'll enter pockets of places that truly feel as they're from another time: weathered one-room school houses with games of stickball being played on dusty diamonds in the play yard, bonnets and suspenders a blur, buggies pulling anything from a cart full of bright orange pumpkins, to tools, to groceries, to families. Get off the beaten path and you'll be rewarded with places selling eggs laid that morning, pies just out of the oven, or quilts crafted right there.

So if you only have a few hours to explore, that's what we recommend; just drive and lose yourself in the bucolic countryside.

If you have more than a few hours, perhaps a few days, we still recommend the drives. But there are also more established activities and places to visit.

It's difficult to visit this part of Ohio and not have an enjoyable experience, but following are some of our suggestions to make the most of your visit.

OF BIKES AND BUGGIES: THE HOLMES COUNTY TRAIL

One of the best ways to see Ohio's largest slice of Amish country is to park your car and pedal on one of the most distinctive bike trails in the USA. The Holmes County Trail is billed as the first of its kind designed specifically to accommodate bikes and buggies. The trail spans much of the Amish archipelago from Killbuck in the south to Fredericksburg in the north (a total of 15 miles, with plans to lengthen it to 29 miles). The trail acts as a direct, safe superhighway for buggy traffic while also providing cyclists with the incredible experience of immersing oneself in the largest Amish and Mennonite settlement in the world. And since the trail is largely on old rail bed it's actually relatively flat, a rarity in hilly Holmes County. The trail consists of two trails running side by side. There is a chip and seal lane which better accommodates horse's hooves and a smooth asphalt lane to better coddle speedy cyclists. The two trails take up about 16 feet at their widest points.

On this trail you'll find yourself sharing space with a tableau from another time: horse-drawn buggies, and crisp, colorful laundry on lines, windmills spinning in the breeze, and herds of cows lazily munching under the noon-day sun. There are several spots along the trail perfect for a picnic and several underpasses provide relief from crossing busy roads.

Signage posted along the trail provides a refresher on sharing the trail with buggies. The trail hub in Millersburg provides an interpretative center, plenty of parking and refreshments, but there is also trail access in Killbuck or Fredericksburg. For information about the latest trail conditions or updates visit **www.holmestrail.org**

The Holmes County Trail feeds into a much larger bike trail network that spider webs across Ohio, that when complete, will connect the state's largest cities:

Cincinnati, Columbus, and Cleveland. You can easily pedal from the Killbuck trail head onto the Mohican Valley Trail. The Mohican Valley Trail is a 4.5 mile span between the Kokosing Gap Trail and the Holmes County Trail. The three trails follow the same former rail corridor.

From the Holmes County trailhead you can easily pedal to the "Bridge of Dreams", Ohio's longest covered bridge at 320 feet. We've observed frequent buggy traffic in this area, both on the bridge and the surrounding roads. The Mohican River rapids swish below. Even if biking isn't your thing, the Bridge of Dreams is still worth a visit. The bridge is off US 62 and there is parking on Hunter Road off of US 62 and you can easily walk onto the covered span.

BERLIN

We recommend using the town of Berlin as your base to explore the Amish Archipelago. Berlin is a quaint town which is an eclectic mix of Amish and English. There definitely is a touristy feel to the town, but we don't find it tacky. There aren't miniature golf courses, waterparks, or outlet malls overwhelming the atmosphere. There are gift shops and candy stores that cater to tourists, but there are also plenty of local places where the Amish shop and go about their day-to-day business. What we love about Zinck's on the Square, 4877 West Main Street, Berlin, OH 44610, phone 330-893-1060, is its affordability and location. You can't beat $69.99 a night and on the occasions we stayed, the clerk knocked off $10 for taking an upstairs room (admittedly many visitors to Berlin are seniors and, well, a flight of stairs may not be appealing). The rooms are clean and functional and, let's face it, you're not going to be spending much time in the room anyway, you'll be

exploring Amish Country! What was such a soothing touch was being serenaded to sleep by the clip-clopping cadence of horse hooves and buggy wheels. The rooms are located near an alley way that a lot of Amish use as a "short-cut" to some nearby doctor's offices and shops, so beginning early in the morning and continuing through evening you get a nice traffic flow of buggies.

Another advantage of Zinck's Inn on the Square is that it is, well, on the square. Berlin can become crowded with cars during peak times so staying at Zinck's allows for an easy walk to most Berlin attractions.

Walk over to **Boyd and Wurthmann,** 4819 East Main Street, Berlin, OH 44610, phone 330-893-3287, for some of their legendary pie. On any given day, depending on the fruit in season, there might be 15 to 20 different varieties on the menu. The restaurant is also not a bad place to eat for breakfast, serving up basic fare. This is not an Amish-owned restaurant, but most of the cooks there are Amish, giving the meals a decidedly Pennsylvania Dutch flair and color.

Accommodations have so much to do with personal preference. If you want to stay in style, there is the more posh Berlin Grande, 4787 Township Road 366, Berlin, OH 44610, phone 330-403-3050. On the other end of the spectrum are quiet bed and breakfasts. We like establishments that are run by Plain people (there aren't many of these) simply because it makes the trip more of a cultural exchange and immersion. Nelson and Ruth Ann Beachy's Sunset View Bed and Breakfast, 4578 Township Road 369, Millersburg, OH 44654, phone 330-893-7902 is located on a quiet road about 2 miles southeast of Berlin. While the name is sunset, we've been to this place at sunrise and it's quiet, unassuming, away from the bustle of Berlin. So if you're seeking solitude and Plainness, this is a good option.

BERLIN AMISH COUNTRY HALF MARATHON AND 5K

The first year for this race was 2012 and it was successful enough for organizers to plan one for 2013 in what will hopefully be an annual event The vast majority of visitors explore Ohio's Amish Archipelago by automobile, but there are few better ways for the physically fit to experience the area than on foot. Held the final Saturday in November (run off some of that turkey and dressing!), the course runs through rural rolling roads in Holmes County where you'll pass Amish schoolhouses, colorful laundry hanging on lines, buggies gently plying the roads, freshly harvested fields, and the colorful burst of changing leaves as autumn wanes. For more information visit **runinohioamishcountry.com**

BERLIN BULK FOOD - This is owned by a New Order Amish family and you'll always receive a friendly greeting while browsing among shelves stocked full of all kinds of bulk foods plus a large selection of fresh cheese, Trail bologna, and other locally made products. It's located at 2 North Market Street, Berlin, Ohio 44610, phone 330-893-2353.

SHARP RUN FARM MARKET, State Route 39 just west of Berlin – We don't usually recommend these types of places, but, sometimes you need a stop for the kids or for the kid in you and while there are a lot of kid-friendly places in Holmes County, perhaps there are none better than Sharp Run. Yes, some of their shtick seems kitschy and over-the-top touristy, but there are several reasons why we like this business.

Lloyd and Edna Miller are the owners of Sharp Run and they are Amish. But they don't advertise that fact, they instead simply want to create a good, wholesome, affordable place for family fun and they succeed on that front. Perhaps the highlight of the year in late summer and fall is the organic corn maze (or maize, as they call it). Sharp Run is located in the heart of the area's Amish commercial country at 5841 State Route 39, Millersburg, OH 44654, phone 330-674-4267. And for the adults, there is always a wide selection of homegrown organic produce on sale.

FARMSTEAD RESTAURANT: The Farmstead Restaurant, 4757 Township Road 366, Millersburg, OH 44654, phone 330-893-4600, is a popular stop for large groups and gatherings. With several buffets offering heaping helpings of hearty Amish-inspired fare, you won't come away hungry. They also have a separate breakfast buffet. We did run into Wanda Brunstetter, a popular author of Amish fiction, once at the lunch buffet. So this is a popular restaurant to see and be seen.

TIME AND OPTICS, 6954 County Road 77, Millersburg, OH 44654, phone 330-674-0210: A drab, non-descript building nestled in the heart of Amish country is the last place one might expect to find a top-of-the-line collection of spotting scopes and Swarovski binoculars, but here they are. Anyone from Ohio's birding elite, including Greg Miller and Kenn and Kimberly Kaufman to newbies to the hobby feel at home here. The first Friday and Saturday in June features the "Optics Fling", an open house where visitors can try equipment before they buy, experience guided birding field trips into the nearby Holmes County hills, and meet "bird luminaries" who come to give talks or sign books.

TROYER'S COUNTRY MARKET, 5201 County Road 77, Millersburg, OH 44654, phone 330-893-3786: If a business isn't Amish owned, we place a premium on establishments that have a lot of Amish customers and by this standard Troyer's fits the bill. Situated on the eastern edge of Berlin, this large bulk food store sells meat, cheese, jams, and jellies and other items in bulk so you can grab a taste of Amish country and take it home with you.

CHARM

As the name implies this village is, well, charming. And there are a fair number of attractions here, but most of them are not Amish-owned and this book focuses on those. Charm is a popular tourist hub and there are some busy places here. Guggisberg Cheese attracts legions of followers with their award-winning cream cheeses and Grandma's Homestead Restaurant with its hearty helpings of comfort food, has many fans. We prefer the charm of Charm, though, to be exploring the surrounding countryside which is some of Ohio's most beautiful (beauty being in the eye of the beholder). A couple of the Amish businesses we like in the Charm area are:

CHARM GIFTS AND NATURES HERBS, 4427 SR 557. 330-893-4516. This is a classic Amish-owned variety store with an emphasis on kitchenwares and, not surprisingly, herbs. Definitely worth a visit.

COUNTRY HILL WOODWORKING,

5494 Township Road 123 – While there are many woodworking business tucked away in the Holmes County hills, this place is worth visiting for the drive alone. You'll pass through old growth forests with red-headed woodpeckers taking flight, past prime Amish farms, and then at the summit of a steep hill is a woodworking shop run by Leroy Miller. Wonderful handcrafted furniture in a small shop made on site, our favorite type of Amish furniture place.

MOUNT HOPE

MRS. YODER'S KITCHEN, 8101 Ohio 241, Millersburg, OH 44654, phone 330-674-0922: There is no better restaurant to experience traditional Amish cuisine than this gem. First of all, it's situated in the center of one of the largest Amish communities in the world. If you want a genuine Amish immersion experience, this is where you'll get it. On any given day for any given meal, half the patrons will be of the Plain persuasion while others are tourists and locals.

Most nights feature two ordering options: off the menu and off the buffet. There's not a buffet every night, but when there is you can sample from such delectable Amish-inspired food like rivvels,

Amish wedding steak, hand-breaded broasted chicken, country-fried steak, and pot roast beef. There are plenty of options for vegetarians as well, including fresh salads created using generations-old recipes and local produce. There are plenty of pies to choose from for dessert, but we recommend the date pudding and cracker pudding. Both of these are traditional Amish desserts.

KIDRON

There's one main reason to come to this tiny Ohio hamlet. No, make that three. Or, what the heck, five: Lehman's, Lehman's, Lehman's, Lehman's, Lehman's! Can you tell We love Lehman's? What started as a sleepy store in a single room to serve the area Amish has morphed into a behemoth offering everything from cookie cutters to kettles. We love to peruse their selection of stoves for heating the home and their kitchenwares sections has everything from hard to find handles for ancient butter churns to 21st century silicon oven-mitts, located at 4779 Kidron Road, Dalton, OH 44618, phone 888-438-5346.

When we visited the Cast Iron Cafe, located in Lehman's, we found the offerings sparse. There was nothing meatless on the menu and much of what was on the menu was typical "snack bar" food. We recommend going across the street to Kidron Pizza, 4692 Kidron Road, Kidron, OH 44636, phone 330-857-3000, for a more filling meal. You'll need the fuel to spend a couple of hours perusing the store which is divided into themed showrooms: major appliances, for instance, or a whole room devoted to grills from simple Hibachis to the most high-end meat smokers.

Okay, there are other reasons to come to Kidron besides Lehman's. Kidron Country Store, 4959 Kidron Road, Apple Creek, OH 44606, phone 330-857-2131, is an emporium that includes everything from groceries to shoes. Whereas Lehman's is more an 'event' store, Kidron Country Store offers everyday staples.

A restaurant in the basement seems more like a nuclear fall-out shelter than an eatery, but it serves up surprisingly tasty food. We had grilled cheese and fries, but they offer a wide selection of typical lunch fare. Amish construction workers on lunch break eat side by side with tourists and locals. The restaurant specializes in breakfast and lunch fare, offering up portions of plenty at prices that won't leave your wallet in tatters. Prepare for a packed house on Thursday when the generations old Kidron Livestock Auction, 4885 Kidron Road, Apple Creek, OH 44606, phone 330-857-2641, takes place.

DATE PUDDING AND BREAKFAST BURRITOS?

What is traditional Amish cooking anyway? When most of us close our eyes (or pick up our forks) we imagine Amish cooking being simple, scratch-made confections lovingly made from the basics of baking: sugar, flour, eggs, and milk. While this would be an accurate description of Amish cooking, the food can be tough to pigeonhole. As Hispanic culture has spread through rural America (where the Amish generally live) homemade salsas and burritos have caught on in Amish kitchens and made their way onto menus in their restaurants. Other foods that seemingly don't have Amish roots have also been embraced by Plain people and have become favorites. The date pudding popular at Amish weddings and in restaurants is one such example.

"Me and my sister make date pudding a lot for weddings," Edna Schrock, a local Amish woman said, adding that she buys dates from the local Mennonite owned bulk food store.

SUGARCREEK

This is a small town with a Swiss flair.

BEACHY'S COUNTRY CHALET RESTAURANT, 115 Andreas Drive NE, Sugarcreek, OH 44681, phone 330-852-4644: Locals just refer to this place as Beachy's and it is our recommended food stop for those exploring the northeast corner of Tuscarawas County or southern Holmes.

MARBEYO BED & BREAKFAST, 2370 County Rd. 144, Sugarcreek, Ohio 44681. Phone: (330)-852-4533

This charming bed and breakfast has been in operation since 1990. Hosts Mark and Betty Yoder are Beachy Amish Mennonites who run this charming traveler's oasis from their 100 acre working farm. There aren't many opportunities to actually stay at a Plain-owned inn or bed and breakfast. So while this place may lack some of the amenities, it more than makes up for in its bucoclic setting and cutural exchange. Plus, we've heard the breakfast alone is worth the price of admission! Marbeyo only has three guest rooms, so space is limited.

DID YOU KNOW?

Sugarcreek, Ohio is home to *The Budget*. The Budget, 134 Factory Street N, is the main newspaper of the Amish and Mennonite diaspora, The weekly paper helps link Plain people world-wide with news and accounts from each settlement. This newspaper remains a crucial communications tool among the Amish since a large segment still lack phones.

MILLERSBURG

LODGING: Chain motels and bed and breakfasts abound through the Amish Archipelago.

PROVISIONS: Fresh Encounter, 2021 Broad Avenue, Findlay, OH 45840, phone 419-422-4826, is a local grocery store in Kenton that offers a full line of essentials.

FOOD: Plenty of Mom & Pop restaurants in Kenton, no Amish restaurants in the area for meals.

GETTING THERE: From Cincinnati: take I-75 north to

OTHER AREA ATTRACTIONS:

While Millersburg is the county seat, it's more removed from the hub of Amish activity that is found in Berlin and Charm. The Comfort Inn, 1102 Glen Drive, Millersburg, OH 44654, phone 877-411-7400, provides chain comfort for those who prefer that type of place. A hospital serves the area.

One event we really like that can't be put under one specific town because the event rotates locations every couple of years: Family Farm Field Day.

FAMILY FARM FIELD DAY

We like this event because it's an event put on by Amish farmers for the general public, Amish and non-Amish. In 2014, the event will be held at the working farm owned by Reuben and Catherine Yoder, 2517 Township Road 606, Dundee, Ohio. The mission statement of the Family Farm Field Day is "to provide an educational format for grass-based agriculture that: supports low energy and a non-industrial way of farming; encourages family lifestyles that promote cohesive, economical, and healthy rural living skills; and seeks to build morale and enthusiasm in the farming community."

With the agrarian lifestyle of the Amish under constant threat, this event seeks to showcase the importance of small-scale farming. The day-long event is free and there are plenty of kid's activities.

"It's everything from beekeeping to alternative energy. We have a natural resource tent to talk about farmstead trapping, timber walks, bird walks and Indian artifacts and children's activities will include an obstacle course, live farm and exotic animals and different games set up for the kids to keep them occupied," explains one of the Amish organizers of the event "Homemakers can learn about herbal tinctures, pasture poultry, a home gardening panel and cooking."

Food vendors are on hand offering up all sorts of hearty and sweet fare. All food vendors are Amish and all funds raised through food sales benefit Amish parochial schools and special education programs.

PENNSYLVANIA

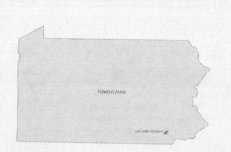

LANCASTER COUNTY

BRIEFLY

This is the oldest and perhaps best-known of all Old Order Amish settlements. We don't devote huge chunks of this book to Lancaster precisely because it has been written about so much.

HISTORY AND INDEPTH INFORMATION

Perhaps more than any other Amish settlement in the USA, Lancaster County is what you make of it. If you want to immerse yourself in history and culture without all the tourist trappings, you can do that. If you want amusement rides and water parks, well, yes, you can do that too. If you want to stay in your car, you can do that and be rewarded with some of the most pristine postcard panoramas in the East. The first time we visited

Lancaster County – over 20 years ago – we elected to see the sights by bicycle and there are plenty of places where you can pedal your way through the the postcard panoramas of Lancaster County.

The first Amish began arriving to the area in the 1720s lured by William Penn's promise of a land of religious tolerance and freedom. After centuries of persecution in Europe, that sounded quite appealing to the embattled pacifist Anabaptist Amish.

The Lancaster County of today is very different from the isolated inland that settlers first found.

The area is now under intense pressure from the ever expanding suburbs of Philadelphia. "Lancaster" is a term that is often used by visitors very broadly. There is the city of Lancaster, which is a charming, history-filled city with a wonderful selection of restaurants and shops. The Amish experience in the city of Lancaster is limited. Most of the time when people say they are visiting Lancaster's Amish communities they are referring to the broad swatch of rural county countryside which is home to the world's second largest Amish population. For the purposes of this book we are lumping Bird-in-Hand, Gordonville, Leola, Paradise and other small settlements under the grouping of Lancaster.

COLONIAL GOAT DIARY, 39 Colonial Road, Gordonville, PA 17529. 717-768-7492. We like this Amish-owned business because they have a retail operation on the family farmstead. For goat cheese lovers this is the place to go! The farm is run by Lester Stoltzfus and the entire operation is organic, non-GMO.

Raw goat's milk and aged cheese, pasteurized fresh goat cheese, on pasture, non-GMO. Directions: 1.5 miles east of Intercourse on Route 340. Left on Colonial Road, 1st farm on right.

BEILER'S FRUIT FARM ,383 Springville Rd., New Holland, PA 17557. 717-354-7228. This is an Amish fruit farm run by Elmer and Barbara Beiler. It's a no-frills market (which is why we like it). It gives you an authentic Amish experience in the heart of Lancaster County. Sells fruits, vegetables, pumpkins, melons, berries, preserves, honey and homemade cider in season.

RIEHL'S QUILTS & CRAFTS, 247 East Eby Road, Leola, Pa 17540: We love Riehl's because it is a slice of simplicity among the tourism miasma of Lancaster County. The quilt store is run, from their working dairy farm, by Sam and Susie Riehl. The store stocks over 200 quilts, Christmas ornaments, jams and jellies, and other goodies almost all locally made either by the Riehl's themselves or other Amish artisans nearby.

ABE'S BUGGY RIDES, 2596 Old Philadelphia Pike, Bird in Hand, PA 17505, phone 717-392-1794: There are several places offering buggy rides and we don't find anything too tacky about wanting the experience. Better let an actual Amish person live their life and go to one of the places offering rides. Not only can you experience the buggy, but you also get a wonderful history tour of the area by guides that generally have Anabaptist roots themselves and know the area and its culture and customs. Lancaster County is in many ways a large living history site. UNESCO has recognized it as a World Wonder. We like the different tour packages offered whether it's a 20 minute countryside quickie or an hour or more tours that stop at an Amish-owned bakery.

ZOOK'S ROADSIDE STAND, 3916 Old Philadelphia Pike, Gordonville, PA 17528, phone 717-768-3349: Tucked among the touristy trappings of Old Philadelphia Pike is a small, unassuming vendor. We like Zook's because despite all the traffic, development and pursuit of bucolic Amish peace in Lancaster County, this place reminds us of one of the typical roadside stands found in less touristy Amish settlements. Here you can peruse the small shop for homemade catsup, apple butter, apple sauce, baked goods, and butter.

WHOOPIE PIE FESTIVAL, held at Hershey Farm Restaurant & Inn, Route 896, Strasburg, PA 17579, phone 717-687-8635, festival date is Saturday, September 6, 2014.

The subject of where Whoopie Pies originated is actually a rather contentious one among food historians. The state of Maine claims its ruggedly independent tradition gave birth to the whoopie pie, while Pennsylvania counters that Amish and Mennonite homemakers concocted the confection. No matter where this scrumptious snack started, it has become synonymous with the Amish.

MUD SALES

Auctions are a staple of Amish life. The events are a great way to raise funds for a good cause and bring the community together. We even have a whole section of this book devoted to showcasing our favorite Amish auctions. But in Lancaster County, auctions are known by a different name, mud sales. And with as much Amish ambiance as Lancaster County offers, if you could only spend a day there and only visit one place or event, we recommend attending a mud sale.

They are great fun and steeped in history and tradition. They derive their name from the fact that the sales have traditionally been held in the early spring when the frozen fields were thawing and the March and April rains were a constant threat. Now there are mud sales throughout the spring, summer, and even fall, but our favorite ones are still in the spring. Bring a good pair of shoes or boots with you because you may have to tromp through a bit of mud on the way to the sale. When you arrive you'll likely find yourself outnumbered 2 – 1 by Amish attendees who are avid supporters of the sales. The sales usually consist of several auctions and a lot of food. As you roam the grounds you'll likely see multiple auctions going on at once; one for produce, one for livestock, one for furniture, one for big-ticket items like appliances or buggies, and one inside the fire station that covers everything and anything else. Some mud sales have over 30 auctions going at once! Even if you don't bid on anything, the sights and sounds are still incredible to take in. And the smells! The amazing aromas of classic Pennsylvania Amish cooking can be found here. There are people who come to the mud sales from far and wide for nothing more than the food.

Each mud sale has their own culinary specialty. At the Bart Township Mud Sale you can munch on a pretzel log roll, which is a pretzel overstuffed with roast beef, sausage, or ham and cheese. There are also homemade, handmade pretzels for sale that you can eat plain or in dip. Sometimes the Bart Township sale sells over 6,000 of these pretzels in a day. The Amish in southeast Pennsylvania have a long tradition of making handcrafted, homemade pretzels.

The Penryn Mud Sale sells overstuffed sausage sandwiches which attract a wide following while the Strasburg sale sells chicken corn soup (a local specialty) by the quart.

In addition to local food favorites, most of the sales have the Amish culinary standbys of homemade doughnuts and barbecued chicken. Much of the food at the sales is Amish made or at the very least, steeped in the centuries-old Pennsylvania Dutch culinary culture.

Unlike Amish auctions elsewhere, these mud sales benefit the local fire department which is, of course, a secular institution, so these aren't "Amish events" per se, but the Amish influence and presence is everywhere. The events are generally not held on Amish homesteads but in fire halls and surrounding grounds. In Lancaster County the Amish have a long-standing tradition of serving as volunteer firefighters. This is not a tradition that has caught on elsewhere, but in Lancaster County some volunteer detachments are primarily Amish with a few token non-Amish needed to drive the emergency vehicles. So the Amish are heavily invested in the fire department and that is why they have such a heavy presence at these sales. At most sales, young Amish boys with wagons will cart your purchases to your car for you in exchange for a tip.

We love these events because they truly are a chance to interact and experience an important part of Amish culture. Food is an important part of this culture and mud sale menus reflect that.

February 23, 2014 - Strasburg Spring Consignment & Mud Sale

8:30 a.m., Strasburg Fire Company #1, 203 Franklin St., Strasburg, PA, phone 717-687-7232. **Sale highlights: Furniture, antiques, quilts, crafts, farm machinery, horses, mules, tools, groceries, fruit, and homemade food.**

March 1, 2014 - Bart Township Annual Auction/Mud Sale

8:30 a.m., Bart Twp. Fire Company, 11 Furnace Road, Quarryville, PA, phone 717-786-3348. **Sale highlights: Antiques, quilts, furniture, new & used equipment, small goods, hay & straw, livestock, buggies, tools, crafts, and food.**

March 8, 2014 - Gordonville Spring Mud Sale & Auction

8:30 a.m., Gordonville Fire Company, Old Leacock Road, Gordonville, PA, phone 717-768-3869. *Sale highlights: This is billed as the largest firemen's auction/sale on the East Coast, featuring 500-600 Amish quilts, antiques, collectibles, new & used furniture, tools, farm equipment, horses, mules, buggies, lawn & garden, barns, utility sheds & trailers, and construction equipment.* A craft show is held the night before from 6 to 9 p.m.

March 15, 2014 - Penryn Fire Company Mud Sale

8:00 a.m., Penryn Fire Company #1, 1441 N. Penryn Road, Manheim, PA, phone 717-664-2825. *Sale highlights: Woodcrafts, furniture, antiques, quilts, crafts, farm equipment, food, and more. Parking will not be available on site.* Satellite parking with shuttle bus service will be available at various neighboring locations.

March 15, 2014 - Airville Mud Sale & Quilt Auction

8:30 a.m., Airville Volunteer Fire Company, 3576 Delta Road, Airville, PA, phone 717-862-3723. *Sale highlights: Quilts, animals (goats, lambs, chickens, rabbits, and roosters), tractors, farm equipment, lumber, household goods, crafts, hay & straw.*

West Earl Mud Sale

8:00 a.m., West Earl Fire Company, PO Box 969, Brownstown PA, phone 717-656-6791 for the 2014 date. *Sale highlights: Handmade quilts and comforters, homemade baked goods, theme baskets, wooden crafts, household items, groceries, lawn & garden equipment, tools, pre-cast concrete, lawn furniture, and more.*

March 21-22, 2014 - Gap Annual Spring Mud Sale/Auction

Friday night craft sale, 5 p.m. Mud Sale Saturday at 8 a.m., Gap Fire Company, 802 Pequea Ave., Gap, PA, phone 717-442-8100. *Sale highlights: Sporting goods, windows & doors, new & used furniture, quilts, crafts, dry goods, groceries, and more.*

April 5, 2014 - Robert Fulton Volunteer Fire Company Mud Sale

8:30 a.m. breakfast, Robert Fulton Fire Company, 2271 Robert Fulton Hwy., Peach Bottom, PA, phone 717-548-8995. *Sale highlights: Crafts, plants, tools, antiques, farm equipment, furniture, food, buggies, wagons, groceries, and horses.*

April 12, 2014 - Rawlinsville Annual Mud Sale

8:30 a.m., Rawlinsville Fire Company, 33 Martic Heights Dr., Holtwood, PA, phone 717-284-3023. *Sale highlights: Antiques, horses, crafts, building materials, lawn equipment, new and used furniture.*

May 10, 2014 - Honeybrook Annual Auction/Mud Sale

7 a.m., Honeybrook Fire Company, 679 Firehouse Lane, Honeybrook, PA, phone 610-273-2688. *Sale highlights: Quilts, crafts, new furniture, Winross diecast model trucks, Smucker's harness and sleigh bells, farm-related supplies, tools, buggies, and heifers.*

June 27, 2014 - Bird-in-Hand Mud Sale | 14th Lancaster County Carriage & Antique Auction

8 a.m., along Rt. 340 (Old Philadelphia Pike) across from Bird-in-Hand Family Restaurant, phone 717-392-0112. *Sale highlights: Antiques, harness and tack, specialty items, quilts, crafts, carriages, buggies, wagons, and food.*

June 28, 2014 - Refton Fire Company Sale

7 a.m. breakfast, Refton Fire Company, 99 Church Street, Refton, PA, phone 717-786-9462. *Sale highlights: Hardware, shop tools, plants, furniture, antiques, crafts, hay and straw, quilts, horses, food, and more.*

August 30, 2014 - Bareville Fire Company Mud Sale

8:30 a.m. breakfast, Bareville Volunteer Fire Company, 211 East Main Street, Leola, PA, phone 717-656-7554. *Sale highlights: Small goods, shop tools, antiques, furniture, lumber, animals, sheds & gazebos, equipment, buggies, concrete items.*

October 25, 2014 -Cochranville Fire Company Mud Sale

7 a.m. breakfast, Cochranville Volunteer Fire Company, 3135 Limestone Road, Cochranville, PA 19330, phone 610-593-5800. *Sale highlights: Tools, household goods, shrubbery, horse tack, quilts, horses, sheds, outdoor furniture, and more.*

TENNESSEE

ETHRIDGE

BRIEFLY

The Amish settlement near Ethridge is notable for several reasons. One, it is the largest Amish community in the Deep South, and it is one of the largest communities of Swartzentrubers in the world. The Swartzentruber Amish are among the most conservative, eschewing indoor plumbing and phones.

HISTORY AND INDEPTH INFORMATION

The land of cotton and sweet tea isn't one usually associated with the Amish. But here in the heart of Tennessee sits an Amish community surrounded by fields of fluffy cotton. The first Amish arrived in Ethridge in 1944 from a now vanished community near the Mississippi gulf coast. Ethridge proved to be just close enough to the Amish areas of the Midwest to keep everyone close and connected to family elsewhere, but far enough to live in agrarian isolation.

The town of Ethridge isn't much more than a collection of buildings and businesses clustered along US Route 43. The Greyhound bus stop stands out among the sleepy buildings, a much-used link to the rest of the world. Area Amish often travel by Greyhound to visit family elsewhere.

Even the food here is a bit different than other Amish communities. While cinnamon rolls and shoofly pie are still staples, okra, molasses, homemade hush puppies, and corn meal are common here.

One interesting twist to a more southern, agrarian Amish community is that weddings are held usually in November through March. Having a big, often outdoor gathering makes more sense in the temperate south during winter instead of the sizzling, sweat-soaked summer months.

This is a very conservative Amish community and while cameras are welcome in many settlements they are definitely frowned upon here even for photos of buggies or barns. So we recommend leaving your camera out of sight in this community and the only photos will be ones in your memories.

We don't typically recommend guided tours of Amish country, there's so much more you can experience when you just explore yourself, we make an exception with Ethridge. The Amish Welcome Center at 4001 Highway 43 North, Ethridge, TN 38456, phone 931-829-2433, offers 90 minute horse-drawn wagon tours of the community. Tour guides with ties to the settlement narrate the history and culture. The tours stop at a wood shop, basket shop, and cedar lawn furniture business.

While the Ethridge Amish are conservative and often insular when it comes to outsiders, there are a fair number of home-based businesses offering everything from homemade molasses to quilts. Homemade sorghum molasses during the summer is a specialty in this settlement. Buy a jug of it to take home to enjoy on biscuits or as a sugar substitute in recipes.

If you visit here during the summer months, the heat can be sweltering, yet in such a conservative community you want to avoid shorts and sandals if possible.

Another place you'll want to check out is Plain and Simple Quilts, 4111 Highway 43 N, Ethridge, TN 38456. This store offers a showcase of quilts from many different Amish styles. In addition to the quilts they have baskets, Amish dolls, wooden quilt racks, and quilt hangers.

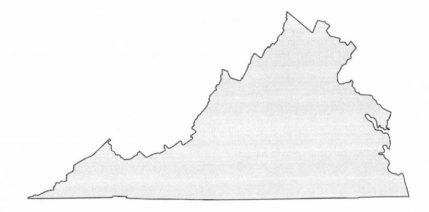

VIRGINIA

DAYTON

GETTING THERE: From I-81 exit 245, go west on Port Republic Road. Go straight through the intersection with Main Street (Route 11). At the next light, turn left onto Route 42 (High Street). Go 3 miles south to Dayton.

LODGING: Plenty of chain motels in nearby Harrisonburg.

PROVISIONS: A Food Lion at 1751 S High Street in Harrisonburg provides all the essential staples.

FOOD: The Dayton Farmer's Market, 3105 John Wayland Hwy., Dayton, VA 22821, phone 540-879-3801, offers a wide selection of locally made lunches, some Mennonite made. Thomas House, 222 Main Street, Dayton, VA 22821, phone 540-879-2181, serves up scrumptious home cooking. Jim's Drive-In, 360 College Street, Dayton, VA 22821, phone 540-879-9156, features American fare, while La Casita, 270 Dingledine Lane, Dayton, VA 22821, phone 540-879-2455, has authentic Mexican food.

OTHER ATTRACTIONS: Visit the Silver Lake Mill, 2328 Silver Lake Road, Dayton, VA 22821, phone 540-879-3582. This historically significant structure has been a central part of Dayton for most of its history. The Silver Lake Mill actively milled flour from its inception in 1822 until 1996 when it was bought and converted into a gift shop and art studio.

Shenandoah National Park, Stanley, VA 22851, phone 540-999-3500, is only an hour away across the valley. Explore some of the highest mountains in the south by traveling on gorgeous, stately Skyline Drive.

EDITOR'S CHOICE: Our first choice is the rustic Skyland Lodge high up in the Shenandoah Mountains. Enjoy the mountains, explore nearby Harrisonburg and then make a day of the Old Order Mennonite community outside of Dayton. The Skyland Lodge is located at mile 41.7 on Skyline Drive, Shenendoah National Park, V, 22835, phone 5540-999-2211

BRIEFLY

The Old Order Mennonites are a pastoral presence in the Shenandoah Valley outside of Dayton, Virginia. The Old Order Mennonites here generally do not speak a dialect of Pennsylvania Dutch as they do in other areas.

HISTORY AND INDEPTH INFORMATION

The Dayton community is a Mennonite microcosm, with three different groups populating the valley: Horning, Wenger, and Stauffer. Don't think the last names will help you. There are Stauffers who are Wengers and Wengers who are Stauffers.

The Wenger and Stauffer Mennonites are both conservative horse and buggy groups who split over relatively minor differences. The Horning Mennonites are also a Plain group but they have adopted the automobile. For a number of years they were known locally as the "black bumper Mennonites" because of their dark-colored cars.

Your first stop should be Burkholder's Buggy Shop, 795 Mason Street, Dayton, VA 22821, phone 540-879-9260, the main source of the area's transportation. But it's not just Mennonites he services. People who need buggies for parades or various collectors also count Burkholder's craftsmanship among the best. Pick up a map from Burkholder's of the area's Mennonite settlement with businesses of note conveniently marked. And then begin on your driving tour of one of the most beautiful Plain settlements anywhere.

Rocky Cedar Enterprises, 2156 Country Store Lane, Dayton, VA 22821, phone 540-879-9714, is much more interesting than the name implies. This is a sundry store started by two Mennonite sisters. You can truly find a bit of everything here but sewing supplies are a specialty. They also have an excellent selection of books. And while you'd think their location tucked away in the valley, far off any interstate, would dampen their business, on days that we visited the parking lot was always bustling with customers coming and going.

Martin Harness Shop, 2659 Harness Shop Road, Dayton, VA 22821, phone 540-879-9302, is an interesting place to stop by. The shop is located in a small outbuilding framed by a beautiful mountain backdrop. The store is packed with saddles, leather, buckles, and anything else an equine fan might want.

As with so many Plain settlements half the joy is the journey. Use the map you got at Burkholder's Buggy Shop to explore the back roads that crease this valley. Be sure to drive up the Molehill, a topographical anomaly in the generally flat valley. The perfectly round mound of the Mole Hill is actually the remnants of an ancient volcano, the last active such hot spot east of the Mississippi. But don't worry, the Mole Hill last erupted over 40 million years ago.

Cycling is an excellent way to see the Valley. The Old Order Mennonites allow bicycles and you'll see plenty of pedal power on display. You can enjoy it yourself by stopping at Mole Hill Bikes, 440 Main Street, Dayton, VA 22821, phone 540-879-2011, to rent.

No visit to the Dayton is complete without stopping at the Dayton Farmers Market, 3105 John Wayland Hwy, Dayton, VA 22821, phone 540-879-3801, which locals affectionately call the "Mennonite Mall." Here you'll find an array of shops from a Mennonite-owned electric and lighting store to a book store (Books of Merit) to a bake shop. Books of Merit, the bookstore, offers a wireless internet signal that bounces around the mall just in case someone needs to be connected.

The signature event of the year here is the Dayton Autumn Celebration which showcases the area's artistry and beauty. The fall fete is held the first Saturday in October where you immerse yourself in the culture, art, and handmade crafts of over 300 vendors.

PEARISBURG

OTHER: Be sure to fuel up your car in either Pearisburg or Dublin, because there are no gas stations between the Amish settlement and these communities.

FOOD: Verona's Pizzeria & Italian Restaurant, 222 Cleburne Blvd., Dublin, VA 24084, phone 540-674-4441, offers a wide selection of traditional Italian fare.

IMPORTANT AT-A-GLANCE INFORMATION

AFFILIATION: New Order Amish; Mennonite.

LODGING: Best bet for exploring the surrounding area is to stay in Dublin, about 20 miles away. There simply aren't many accommodations closer to the Amish community.

PROVISIONS: There is a Food Lion, 302 South Main Street, Pearisburg, VA 24134, phone 540-921-2571, and a Rite Aid, 121 North Main Street, Pearisburg, VA 24134, phone 540-921-1284, that sell basic provisions. A Dairy Queen, 503 North Main Street, Pearisburg, VA 24134, phone 540-921-1476, provides a place to grab a quick snack.

GETTING THERE: From Dublin, Virginia take State Route 100 20 miles to State Route 460 West. Travel approximately 10 miles and follow signs to the various Amish stores.

EDITOR'S CHOICE: Verona's Pizzeria and Italian Restaurant, 222 Cleburne Blvd., Dublin, VA 24084, phone 540-674-4441, offers a great selection of hearty Italian fare after exploring the Amish community.

BRIEFLY

This Amish community is one of the most remote settlements in the USA. It goes by several names. Some refer to it as the Pearisburg community (which is actually 20 miles away, but it is the postal address), others call it the "White Gate" settlement, named after a nearby tiny hamlet by the same name. Still, others call it the "Walker Mountain" community, which may be the most accurate moniker of all since the Amish live on the slope of this gently rising peak.

HISTORY AND INDEPTH INFORMATION

The Pearisburg community is not your typical Amish settlement. Horse-drawn buggies are a rarity on the roads, as most church members live in close proximity. The settlement draws its inspiration from some Amish elders who have espoused a more communal way of living. This small church district has also been roiled by theological divisions. As of this writing some Amish had aligned themselves with a Plain church in Lobelville, Tennessee. They identify themselves as Mennonite. The Lobelville Mennonite men have mustaches, a characteristic rarely seen in any Plain church.

Visitors during the summer should keep an eye out for the once-a-month bake sale and lunch held to raise funds for the Walker Mountain School. An $8 meal includes a generous helping of chicken, two side dishes, a slice of bread, and dessert. Seating for the meal is held inside the school. In addition to the meal, a bake sale is conducted where one can buy homemade doughnuts, whoopie pies, bread, and even hand-cranked ice cream. The day prior to the meal you'll find the schoolhouse filled with the bustle of Amish community members churning out fresh baked pecan and apple pies and getting everything ready for the hundreds of visitors.

If you aren't lucky enough to score one of the schoolhouse meals, there is still plenty to see and do in the White Gate community. Three days a week during the growing season there is a farmer's market on Mountainview Lane. You never know what you'll find there, from plump red tomatoes to pastries and noodles. Call ahead to check hours, Jessie Miller: 540-921-2466, extension 3 (call for days/hours confirmation).

The first place any visitor to Walker Mountain should check out is the Nature Way Country Store. It's a traditional, old-fashioned Amish-run general store offering deli sandwiches, homemade ice cream, bulk foods, herbs, spices, dried fruits, nuts, canned goods, baked goods, eggs, meats, and cheeses. Nature Way Country Store is located at 106 Nature Lane, Pearisburg, VA 24134 and is open most days from 8 a.m. to 5 p.m. Call ahead at 540-921-1381, extension 1, to check hours. Another place to check out is Mountain View Country Store, 287 Songbird Lane, Pearisburg, VA 24134, phone 540-921-4308. Run by Katie and Dan Wengerd, their specialty is Amish style clothing, fabrics, and sewing materials.

Forget the big box furniture stores. The Walker Mountain settlement is home to Heritage House Handcrafted Furniture, 265 Mountain View Lane, Pearisburg, VA 24134, phone 540-921-2466, offering a wide array of hand-made Amish furniture from the community. Meanwhile, check out the local harness and tack shop run by Jonathan Hershberger on White Pine Road, Pearisburg, VA, phone 540-921-5202, extension 2.

WISCONSIN

WISCONSIN

IMPORTANT AT-A-GLANCE INFORMATION

AFFILIATION: Old Order Amish (traditional)

EDITOR'S CHOICE: Sloping Acres Greenhouse, W4376 Highway 44, Markesan, WI 53946; Salemville Cheese Coop, W4481 Highway GG, Cambria, WI 53923, phone 920-394-3433.

BRIEFLY: Not to be Wisconsin cliché, but this is "cheese country", so if curds and whey are your thing, you've come to the right place! But this is also the "land of greenhouses." While we've seen greenhouses aplenty in many Amish settlements, this seems to be the land of the "emerald thumb."

CAMBRIA-DALTON-PARDEEVILLE

HISTORY AND INDEPTH INFORMATION

Visiting the Amish in this slice of central Wisconsin's "dairy belt" bears a strong resemblance to northern Indiana's Amish. Many families moved to the area to take advantage of less crowds and cheaper farmland. The first families began moving to this bucolic patch of dairy land in the late 1970s Now around 350 families live in nine sprawling church districts.

No visit to the Dalton Amish settlement is complete without stopping at Mishler's Country Store, W 5115 Barry Road, Dalton, WI 53926, phone 608-429-3392, a typical bulk food emporium selling everything from sugar and spices to cookbooks and chocolate-covered pretzels. Mishler's is located seven miles north of Pardeeville on Hwy.

22 to Barry Road, then east two miles. You'll share the shop with plenty of Amish who use Mishler's as their main grocery store. Do make a note that Mishler's is closed on Thursdays. We saw a cheeky sign in Mishler's parking lot by the hitching posts that said "ENERGY EFFICIENT: HORSES ONLY. VEHICLE RUNS ON OATS AND GRASS. CAUTION! DON'T STEP IN THE EXHAUST!" As the sign indicates you'll find the Amish here, like most anyplace, being warm and welcoming.

We stopped at the Shady Lane Variety Store on Barry Road, Dalton, WI 53946, not far from Mishler's. Here we bought a board game for some Amish friends back home. As the name implies, Shady Lane stocks a range of tough to find items.

This Amish community consists of about 350 families with members of 50 families involved in the milk production and the cheese making. Salemville cheese is a true co-op and let me tell you, the cheese-making is centered in an unassuming building at County Trunk Highway Gg outside of Cambria. But inside this unassuming building is cheese magic being made, specifically blue cheese.

CANADA

CANADA

AYLMER

IMPORTANT AT-A-GLANCE INFORMATION

LODGING: For those who prefer more chain-oriented accommodations there is a Comfort Inn 15 minutes away in St. Thomas at 100 Centennial Avenue, St. Thomas, Ontario N5R 5B2, Canada, phone 1-519-633-4082. For closer quarters to the Amish settlement outside of Aylmer, we recommend Pinecroft, 8122 Rogers Road, Aylmer, Ontario N5H 2R4, Canada, phone +1-519-773-3435.

AYLMER

PROVISIONS: A Valu Mart at 125 N. John Street, Aylmer, Ontario N5H 2A7, Canada, phone +1-519-773-9219, carries a full line of groceries for any picnicking or lunch-packing. We also like the ubiquitous Canadian chain, Shopper's Drug Mart at 6 Talbot St E., Aylmer, Ontario N5H 1H4, Canada, phone +1-519-765-1088. This store carries staples and provisions needed for your stay.

BRIEFLY

Aylmer is one of Canada's largest and best-known Amish settlements.

HISTORY AND INDEPTH INFORMATION

We joked that we should have named this book from Pinecroft to Pinecraft because, really, what are the odds of staying in a bed & breakfast called Pinecroft and then staying in an Amish settlement called Pinecraft (see page 25)?

Pinecroft is on the opposite side of Aylmer from the sprawling Amish settlement on the north side of town, but the quaint bed & breakfast and pottery outlet still offers a comforting base from which to explore.

What you'll notice in Aylmer more so than any other Plain settlement is the presence of a "Mennonite melting pot." The Amish community is easily identified by their horse and buggies and beards, but there is also a vibrant community of Mennonites. Russian Mennonites and Mennonites who have moved back to Canada from Mexico both add an ethic flavor to this Plain settlement. Aylmer has a quaint, old-fashioned downtown. The province of Ontario's tax on plastic shopping bags has made even the most eco-lax person into an environmentalist. You'll see Plain people strolling downtown with reusable shopping bags.

A good starting point is visiting the Aylmer Sales Arena, 51 Murray Street, Aylmer West, Ontario, N5H 2A55, Canada, phone +1-519-765-2211, a Farmers and Flea Market open every Tuesday from 8 a.m. to 4 p.m. While much of it is just typical flea market fare, there is a Plain presence with meat, cheese, and baked good vendors.

A great place to put on your Aylmer itinerary is the HOPE Eco Farm owned by Amish man Franz Seeberger. A small shop is on the premises that sells freshly milled flour, all organic and stoneground, as well as honey. And what is also interesting is that Franz can connect visitors of his shop with other Amish farmers in the community who sell organic vegetables and meat and eggs for example.

The Amish don't use internet and therefore don't have a webpage but the farm is always available during the daytime at 10737 Walker Road, Aylmer, Ontario, Canada and Franz also has a voice mail at +1-519-765-1031, ext. 3. If you leave your number, Franz Seeberger returns your call.

If he's not too swamped when you drop by, he's very generous with his time in showing how the milling process works.

Pathway Publishing is headquartered here in Aylmer and is where such Amish staples as Family Life, Young Companion, and Blackboard Bulletin are published. The tiny, unassuming brick building that houses Pathway occupies an important part of Amish intellectual and religious culture. The publishing house was started in the 1960s by David Wagler and Joseph Stoll who thought that the Amish lacked a source of their own literature. You can stop in during business hours (it is located on Rural Route 4, Aylmer, Ontario N5H 2R3, Canada).

LINDSAY

This is probably the farthest north Amish settlement we've been to, although it's not too far off the same latitude that Unity, Maine (see page 98) is located. But climate-wise it sure feels like it is in the polar climes, especially if you do what we did and visit during the dead of winter.

The Lindsay Amish community is a wonderful opportunity for those in Greater Toronto to experience Amish culture. While the settlement bills itself as Lindsay, it is actually about 20 minutes north of this quaint Canadian town in an area known as Kawartha Lakes.

Zehr's Farm Fresh Produce & Bakery, 1690 Glenarm Road, RR #3, Woodville, Ontario, K0M 2T0, Canada.

Fresh Taste Bakery Naturipe Produce, 463 Mark Road, Cameron, Ontario D0M 1G0, Canada.

◢ MENNONITE RELIEF SALES

Mennonite Relief Sales are held in 45 different locations throughout the United States each year. The sales raise funds for the Mennonite Disaster Service which dispatches teams of Mennonite and Amish assistance to areas impacted by natural or man-made tragedy. The relief sales are part festival, part charity, part sale, and part amazing food experience. Everyone comes away feeling good. There are several festivals where the Plain participation is high. Old Order Amish and Plain Mennonites participate heavily in the sales in Kansas, Indiana, Illinois, and Ohio. At sales where the Amish presence is high, the menu reflects it. The Michiana Mennonite Relief sale features breakfast haystacks (an Amish classic), pulled pork sandwiches, pancakes and sausage, apple butter, apple fritters, and many other traditional favorites.

INDIANA: Michiana Mennonite Relief Sale, Elkhart County 4H Fairgrounds, 17746 County Road 34, Goshen, IN 46528. This sale is in the heart of northern Indiana's Amish Country. The sale is held the final week of September with festivities kicking off on Friday evening at 5 p.m. and continues the whole following day. Here's a sample schedule courtesy of the Michiana Mennonite Relief Sale:

Friday, September 26, 2014

5:00 p.m. - 9:00 p.m.

- Silent Auction
- Children's Auction begins at 6:30 p.m.
- Haystack Supper

- Most food booths open

- Baked goods for sale

- Ten Thousand Villages / Crafts selling items all evening

- Men's Chorus begins at 7 p.m.

- Run for Relief registration for Saturday Run/Walk

- Fair Trade Coffee House w/Live Entertainment

Saturday, September 27, 2014

7:00 a.m. to mid-afternoon

- Pancake & Sausage Breakfast begins at 7 a.m.

- Breakfast Haystacks begin at 7 a.m.

- Garage Sale items begin at 7 a.m.

- Run for Relief begins at 8 a.m.

- Silent Auction building open 8 a.m. – 1 p.m.

- Pickup items won in the silent auction 1:30-3 p.m.

- Quilt Auction begins at 8 a.m.

- New & Used Auction not happening this year

- Ten Thousand Villages / Crafts selling items all day

- All food booths are open and baked goods are sold.

OHIO: The annual Relief Sale takes place the first Friday & Saturday of August every year. Friday afternoon at 4:00 p.m. food is available and the booths are open; the evening program begins at 6:30 p.m. Then at 7:00 a.m. Saturday morning, breakfast is served. The 5K Run and Walk start at 8:00 a.m. The art and collectible auction starts at 9:00 a.m. along with the wood auction. The quilt auction starts at 10:00 a.m. The sale is located at Buckeye Event Center, 624 Henry Street, Dalton, Ohio 44618. (Source: Ohiomccreliefsale.org)

Other relief sales with a Plain presence include:

Kansas Mennonite Relief Sale

State Fair Road

Hutchinson, KS 67502

620-747-2245

The Kansas Mennonite Relief Sale is held the second Friday and Saturday in April.

Gap Relief Auction, 172 South Lime Street, Quarryville, PA 17566, phone 717-687-9470. This auction will next be held August 8 and 9, 2014.

◢ SHORT STOPS

This is not intended to be a directory of every single Plain-owned store in the USA. That could be quite a lengthy book! These are just some we can recommend because we've been there or know of people who have. Look for expanded listings in future editions of this book. We can't necessarily recommend planning a whole trip around these places, but they are worth a stop.

We love Plain-owned bulk food stores. But we also want to be clear, we believe the best Amish experiences come from visiting home-based businesses. There's nothing better than following a hand-lettered sign for "fresh brown eggs," driving down a long, gravel-covered driveway, past lazily munching cows in a field, through the fresh ruts of buggy wheels, and pulling up to a century-old farmhouse to buy eggs, produce, or crafts straight from the source. And often you'll make a new friend in the process.

Most Amish settlements have bulk food stores. The lay-out of each store is similar and many of their goods are similar. But there is usually local flavor to be found, and that's what we really like about the bulk food stores. Often these stores are "community hubs" where you'll find information (bulletin boards with fliers or just word-of-mouth) about upcoming auctions, benefit suppers, or other Amish-owned businesses. These stores are a great way to get a feel for a community and to stock up on reasonably priced staples in bulk.

To find the local flavor, look for the baked goods. Many of these stores either have an in-house bakery where they serve local favorites, whether it's chocolate shoo-fly pie in Pennsylvania or sugar cream pie in Indiana or a baked goods table where fresh doughnuts and bread are brought in. Some of these stores also have delis where fresh, locally prepared salads and sandwiches are made. So visit and enjoy these bulk food stores, but always try to use them as your jumping off point to explore the surrounding back roads. Here are some of our favorite Amish, Mennonite, or Brethren-owned bulk food stores:

FLORIDA

HOMESTEAD: Knauss Berry Farm, 15980 SW 248th Street, Homestead, FL 33031, phone 305-247-0668: This is a German Baptist-owned bakery and produce stand serving South Florida since the 1950s. The bakery has legions of fans who shop for the outstanding produce and fresh flowers, fruit flavored milkshakes and homemade ice cream. Strawberry shakes are a specialty, and the cinnamon rolls also have a cult following. Knauss Berry Farm is only open from Nov 1 through mid-April, so plan accordingly. Lines for their famous cinnamon rolls can snake into the parking lot. The bakery is open 8 a.m. to 5:30 p.m. Monday – Saturday, of which Saturday's being particularly busy.

ILLINOIS

Flat Rock: New Order Amish-owned Villas County Store, 10282 E 340th Avenue, They have a good assortment of bulk foods, baking supplies, and deli.

INDIANA

Montgomery: David Waglers Quilts 4413 E 200 N Montgomery, IN 47558 (812) 486-3836. A must-stop for the home quilter, an Amish-owned business full of needlepoint and quilt supplies!

Rosebud: New Order Amish-owned Shoppers Discount Surplus Grocery, 6321 SW Washington School Road, Salem, IN, phone 812-883-8016.

Livonia: Dutch Barn, 383 East Main Street, Highway 56, Livonia, IN 47108, phone 812-755-5161. You will find furniture, housewares, bulk food, and deli.

Paoli: Harness Shop and Variety Store, 4481 N County Road 300 W. They sell baked goods, kitchenware, herbs, books, and toys.

Vevay: Dutch Discount, 1722 Hwy 56, Vevay, IN, phone 812-427-2594. This Amish-owned bulk food store also sells crafts and baked goods.

IOWA

Orchard: Stillwater Greenhouse, 3110 Shadow Avenue, Mennonite-owned, with a large selection of greenhouse plants, mixed containers, garden decor and more.

KENTUCKY

Cub Run: Detweiler's Country Store, 12825 Priceville Road (Highway 728), Cub, Run, KY 42729, phone 270-524-7967. You really get two stores for the price of one here. This Old Order Amish-owned business has two buildings on the same lot. One is an old-time, old-fashioned hardware store specializing in those hard to find items in the hardware category, plus feed and farm supplies. The country store stocks everything from jigsaw puzzles and singing clocks to clothing, food supplies, and baked goods. The deli provides made-to-order sandwiches. Detweiler's

Country Store is open Monday through Friday, from 8 a.m. to 5 p.m. (Central Time), and from 8 a.m. to 4 p.m. on Saturday, closed on Sunday.

Stephensport: Mennonite-owned Kountry Korner Market, 12730 N Highway 259, Stephensport, KY 40170, phone 270-547-2021.

Owenton: Country Side Bakery is a Mennonite bulk food store, bakery, and deli on at 4758 U.S. 127, Owenton, KY 40359, phone 502-484-3323. They specialize in doughnuts, baked goods, bulk foods, and spices. Customers love their freshly made doughnuts. A homemade pumpkin roll sold year-round is also popular. This bakery is owned by the Stoltfus family.

An unusual aspect of this bulk food store is the music which is piped in over the store's speaker system, sort of a blend of Swiss yodeling and gospel music, a nod to the heritage of the Mennonite community here. This particular settlement is comprised of a small sect of Mennonites known as "The Ambassadors", a branch of the Beachy Amish Mennonite church.

Cynthiana: Grandview Country Market, 9216 US Highway 27 N, Cynthiana, KY 41031, phone 859-234-0505, is a Mennonite-owned bulk food store and bakery. They sell an array of spices, deli items, and homemade baked goods.

MICHIGAN

Charlotte: Amish-owned J & L Country Store, 5757 W. Kinsel, Charlotte, MI 48813, phone 517-541-0575. They specializes in supplies and sundries.

Homer: Amish-owned Countryside Bakery & Bulk Foods, 2204 29 Mile Road, Homer, MI 49245. The store is open Monday thru Saturday 8 a.m. - 6 p.m.

Homer: Amish-owned Royal Oak General, 27925 P Drive South, Homer, MI 49245, phone 517-568-5983. This is an old fashioned General Store in Homer's Amish community.

Snover: Mennonite-owned Country View Bulk Foods, 177 N Germania Road, 1/4 mile north of 46, between M-53 and M-19, Snover, MI 48472, phone 989-635-3764. Country View specializes in fresh fruits and vegetables, general groceries and bulk foods, with a large selection of cheeses - sliced, block, pre-packaged, bulk, and spices and baking supplies.

MONTANA

EDITOR'S CHOICE - GOLD CREEK: We are excited to recommend this place because occasions to dine in Plain-owned eateries are rare. Not far off Interstate 90 between Missoula and Butte is the small Plain community of Gold Creek. This is a Mennonite settlement and if you're able to make your schedule work be sure to stop at The Dinner Bell on Thursday nights. These weekly suppers are all-you-can-eat for $13.50 and typically draw 100 or so people. The first Thursday night of each month a sumptuous meatloaf is served, the other Thursday suppers are chicken. So plan accordingly. All the food is scratch-made. Also on the menu: mashed potatoes and gravy, local vegetables, salad, homemade bread, and pie and ice cream. The meals are served by Marion and Rhoda Sommers and children and they conclude each evening meal with a round of hymns. Reservations to the weekly Thursday night family-style dinner are recommended to secure a spot. Call 406-288-

2579. Dinner is served at 6 p.m. There is also a Dinnerbell store and deli hours are 8 a.m. to 5 p.m. Monday through Friday and 8 a.m. to 3 p.m. Saturday. The store and deli are very much the typical Amish/Mennonite bulk food establishment with a wide arrange of candy and spices.

NEW YORK

Canastota: Ingallside Meadows Farm, 3111 Ingalls Corner Road: This is a farm run by Amish farmer David Kline and his family. The Klines sell pork and beef by the whole or half, available in fall. Organic broiler chickens are sold all summer. The Klines also sell fresh daily supply of eggs. Open for customers to visit Monday through Saturday.

OHIO

Clayton: A Bushel and a Peck Bulk Foods, 9515 Haber Road, Clayton, OH, phone 937-836-4997. This German Baptist-owned bulk food store sells an array of spices, snacks, and other edibles, easily accessible off of I-70 west of Dayton.

Clayton: Landes Fresh Meats, 9476 Haber Road, Clayton, OH 45315, phone 937-836-3613. This is a German Baptist-owned business featuring old-time freshly butchered meats from steaks to salmon. A small selection of home-baked goods are also available.

Frankfort: This is a relatively new Mennonite community in Ross County, Ohio. It is a "daughter community" of the Mennonites in Dayton, Virginia (see page 206) begun in 2003. The Old Home Place, 2225 Frankfort Clarksburg Pike, Frankfort, OH 45628, phone 740-998-4303, is a Mennonite owned bulk food and bakery by the Schwartz family.

PENNSYLVANIA

Philadelphia: There aren't many opportunities for Amish country to come to the city, but the Reading Terminal Market is one such rarity. This iconic market features several Amish vendors that come from nearby Lancaster County to sell their wares. The Reading Terminal Market is located at 12th & Arch Streets, contact 215-922-2317 for more information. We recommend Beiler's Bakery for amazing Amish-made cinnamon rolls (that scream cinnamon) and a doughnut experience that keeps fans coming back continually. All Amish vendors operating at Reading Terminal Market are open Tuesdays through Saturday, 8 a.m. to 3 p.m. on Tuesdays and Wednesdays, 8 a.m. to 5 pm. Thursday through Saturday.

Selinsgrove: Weaver's Bakery and Farmer's Market on Route 11 and 15 just south of town. This bakery is run by Stauffer Mennonites and offers a delectable selection of baked goods. Keep a special eye out for their homemade chocolate shoofly pie!

TENNESSEE

Whitesville: Backermann's Bakery & Cheese is located in Whiteville at 260 Highway 64. You may contact them at 731-254-8473. This unassuming bakery owned by a Beachy Amish Mennonite family turns out some great treats. One of our favorites are fresh fry pies (some people call them fried pies). Fried pies are fruit-filled half pies covered in a sugary glaze. Backermann's also offer a selection of homemade breads (jalapeno, cheese, plain white, honey wheat, and rosemary garlic), bulk foods, spices, and a deli. The bakery is run by the Yoder family. Backermann is a German word roughly translated as "baker man".

CANADA

http://www.mennoworld.org/2012/10/29/bed-and-breakfast-offers-taste-amish-mennonite-lif/

The Hidden View Bed and Breakfast near Mount Hope, OH, in the heart of the Ohio Amish country, is a wonderful place to stay. It is run by Noah and Nancy Troyer who are members of the Beachy Amish, who dress plain but have electricity and drive cars.

We have stayed there several times and fully recommend it. The B&B is a building separate from the farm and comprises two double bedrooms, one with a bathroom en suite and the other has its own bathroom, too. Noah will come across in the evenings and entertain you with puzzles of various kinds, which are fascinating. If you are there on Sunday, they will probably invite you to go to church with them: they also entertained us with Sunday lunch. Brilliant!

There is a large living room/kitchen in the B&B building. Each day, Nancy brings over something home baked for breakfast but the cupboards are well stocked with everything you would want, too. Don't expect radio or TV, though! Just a five minute drive away is Mrs. Yoder's Restaurant, a great place to eat and very popular.

◢ AUCTIONS & SUPPERS

For a genuine cultural experience, we love attending Amish auctions! First of all, it's a time when non-Amish and Amish alike mix and mingle to pursue a common cause, whether that is raising money for a local school fund or a relief benefit. The school auctions are enjoyable because it's a happy occasion, there's usually plenty of Amish-made food being served and there are usually a wide range of items being sold from maybe a $10 hand-made wooden ornament to $1,000 quilts. Here are a few of our favorite Amish auctions. This list is by no means meant to be a comprehensive list of all the Amish auctions. This is just meant to be a sampling highlighting some of our favorites. Be sure to visit the **thewilliamsguide.com** for updated auction lists and additions.

ILLINOIS

EDITOR'S CHOICE - Robinson: A couple of times a year the Amish settlement in nearby Flat Rock serves suppers which are available on a freewill basis as a fund-raiser to pay medical bills for church members. These fund-raisers are held once or twice a year at the Robinson Community Center at 300 South Lincoln Street in Robinson, Illinois. Meat varies mashed potatoes, gravy, noodles, vegetables, tossed salad, white wheat bread , pepper bread, apple butter, church peanut butter spread and pies. The next meal is on a Friday evening in March 2014. Call Robinson City Hall at 618-544-7616 for information.

INDIANA

CANAAN: This is a Swiss Amish community in southern Indiana. This settlement hosts a semi-annual consignment auction which benefits the local Amish school. It is at 244 Popular Ridge Road, Canaan, IN 47224. Call 812-689-6283 for more information.

MILROY: This is one of the older auctions we know of. The Milroy, Indiana Amish auction (semi-annual) first launched in 1959 and continues to go strong, billing itself as a consignment auction, bake sale, and quilt sale all rolled into one. Five different auction rings are going simultaneously, with festivities beginning at 9 a.m. on the final Saturday of August. A lunch-stand serves up Amish-made goodies throughout the day. We like that this auction is held at the school house that it benefits, it's kind of neat for someone who has never had the chance to see an Amish school. The address is 900 South St., Rd. 3 in Milroy, IN. Call Menno Schwartz Auction service for more information at 317-538-6885.

OHIO

ANDOVER: Benefit sale is usually held the last Saturday of July on Noah J. Yoder's farm at 2405 Pymatuning Lake Road, Andover, Ohio. Starting at 9 a.m., the sale features household items, tools, farm equipment, etc. The quilt sale starts approximately 10:30 a.m. They also serve breakfast and lunch as well as having a bake sale and ice cream. Sale conducted by Orus Mast, auctioneer 330-359-0721.

CONNEAUT: This benefit sale is usually held the first Saturday of August on Dan & Anna Shetler's farm at 6742 Hildom Road, Conneaut, Ohio, beginning at 9 a.m. This is not a school auction, but rather an annual community benefit to raise money to pay for medical bills for any needy in the Amish community. The settlement consists of over 70 families. The auction features quilts, household goods, and farm machinery. As usual, one could also come just for the food which consists of Amish baked goods with barbecued chicken and ice cream. Some years this event has also featured homemade pizza, and scratch-made doughnuts, which are always a hit. Sale conducted by Bob Fink Auction Service, 440-858-2260.

HILLSBORO: We love this auction! There are awesome deals on furniture, hand-crafted Amish-made furniture produced right there in the community. Also, the auction features hand-made quilts, furniture, farm implements, buggies, and other assortments. Food is served and that's enough to draw many people even if they don't come to bid. About 500 bid cards are usually handed out and 750 pounds of chicken are barbecued to feed the crowd according to organizers. The auction is held at 11861 Karnes Road, Greenfield, OH 45123. Call 937-446-4455 for more information.

MIDDLEFIELD: A Traditional Amish Auction held the second Friday of October, 4:00 pm - finished, at the Middlefield Market Pavillion, 15848 Nauvoo Road, Middlefield, OH 44062, free admission and parking, fabulous food stands and bake sale, large silent auction, live auction to include Amish made quilts, furniture and crafts, for more information call 440-632-1668.

MINNESOTA

ST. CHARLES: A consignment auction is held the third Saturday in May to benefit the local Amish schools. Highlights include the sale of driving and riding horses, draft horses, ponies, carriages, tack, furniture, and wood-crafts. From St. Charles, MN take Hwy. 74 south approximately one mile to county road 35, go east to T, turn right at T and go 1/4 mile. Auction is on the right side, 13473 County Road 35, St. Charles, MN 55972. A pancake breakfast begins at 7 a.m. The auction begins at 9 a.m.

WADENA: This is a large full day auction selling two auction rings most of the day with consignments of horses and horse related equipment, farm/ranch related items, vintage and antique items, collectibles, plus a large selection of quilts and fancy work, handmade furniture and more. This auction is held annually in the Spring and Fall with proceeds used for the Amish Schools. Come and enjoy a homemade donut and buy some bake goods, there is also a large bake and lunch sale throughout the day. Call Aasness Auctioneers for details at 218-589-8598.

OKLAHOMA

CLARITA: The Amish women of the Clarita community work year-round crafting quilts for their annual parochial school auction held the second Saturday each September. The hand-stitched, colorful quilts are the big attraction of this auction. In addition to auction items, this auction has actual craft booths set up so you buy directly from vendors. All food booths are Amish-run and all meals are made by the local Amish community including the early Saturday morning sausage and pancake feed, along with home-made ice cream, bread, pies, and cakes. The auction is held at a different farm each year in Ash Township. For general information about the auction call Floyd Bontreger at 580-428-9200.

PENNSYLVANIA

GENESEE: On the third Saturday of August, the small Amish settlement around the town of Genesee holds its annual auction to benefit the local parochial school. The auction started in 2006 and features furniture, quilts, livestock, sheds, and housewares. Amish-prepared barbecued chicken is a big draw along with an accompanying bake sale. The auction is held at Schawartz Metal Roofing & Siding, 1110 Collins Hill Rd, Genesee, PA.

GRATZ: While we prefer Amish auctions that are held on a farmstead or at a school, this auction is so large that it is spread out over two days and is held at the county fairgrounds. This annual auction is held the first weekend (Friday and Saturday) of October and goes to benefit the Amish schools in the lower Northumberland region. Day one of the auction is all about horses. A horse tack auction begins at 6 p.m. followed by an equine auction at 7 p.m. You can arrive at the fairgrounds as early as 8 a.m. if you are bringing horses. And at 1 p.m. Amish-made barbecued chicken wings and ribs are served. There is also kettle cooked ham and bean soup on Friday's menu. Saturday features all-day auctions starting on the hour. The auctions have themes ranging from lawn furniture to lumber to coal stoves. New furniture, quilts, and crafts are one of the most popular auctions, which begins at 9 a.m. Saturday's menu includes an all you can eat breakfast buffet, pig roast, barbecued chicken, and plenty of Amish-baked goods. Questions about the auction can be directed to 570-758-3388.

LOYSVILLE: This is pretty much your typical Amish auction, which is why we like it. But we also like the food selection: authentically Pennsylvania Amish. There are local specialties like elderberry pie and chicken corn soup served. Buggies and quilts and other interesting items are on the auction block. Call Ephraim at 717-438-3970 for more information. The auction location is 531 Iron Bridge Road, Loysville, PA 17074, and is held the second Saturday of July. Proceeds go to benefit the Amish school.

NEWBURG: This Amish school auction launched in 1975 and is still going strong the second Saturday of May. Quilts, crafts, and some livestock are on the auction block. This auction is larger than some because it benefits several surrounding Amish school districts. Four separate auction rings are going simultaneously and Amish cooks bring in two mobile commercial kitchens to serve up all kinds of goodies. Grilled chicken is a big draw to this auction, which is held in an Amish family's timber-framing warehouse at 15700 Burnt Mill Road, Newburg, PA. Call 717-423-6438 for more information.

TURBOTVILLE: The third Saturday of April and the second Saturday of September features the twice annual Beaver Run School Auction. This auction uses the proceeds to benefit five Amish parochial schools. Readers report that the homemade doughnuts served here by Amish bakers are "insanely good" and that chicken is being barbecued all day long and is quite tasty. Homemade ice cream is also a popular draw. This is one of the few Amish auctions that do accept credit cards. Fliers passed out describe the many quilts up for auction. We like this auction because it is held at the Beaver Run Amish School so if you've never been to one before, this is a great chance to see the charm up close. This auction also encourages potential bidders and buyers to come the Friday evening before just to see what items are available. No sales are made the Friday evening prior, but it is a fun time to see the items in a more relaxed atmosphere. And there is also food available! Doughnuts, hot dogs, hot sausage sandwiches, and other goodies are sold. The sale begins at 7 a.m. Getting there: Beaver Run Parochial School is 1 mile north of Route 54 between Washingtonville and Turbotville. Call 570-437-3704 for more information.

WISCONSIN

ALBANY: This Amish auction started in 1996 and benefits the Clearview Amish schools. The auction features quilts, woodcraft, furniture, comforters and horse-related items. The auction is held on the grounds of the Amish school located at W114 Atkinson Road, Albany, WI 53502. A bake sale and lunch stand are also offered. The auction begins promptly at 8:30 a.m.

MARION: This is a real neat auction started back in 2004 and held the first Saturday each June. The auction proceeds go to benefit the local parochial school. In addition to an auction, there is also a pancake breakfast prior from 7 a.m. to 9 a.m., along with a school bake sale. Furniture, quilts, and antiques are all up for sale. The auction is held on the Lester Lambright Farm at N10405 Highway 110, Marion, WI 54950.

READSTOWN: The final Saturday of May is the annual craft auction to benefit the local Amish parochial school. The auction begins at 9 a.m., with a pancake breakfast served by the Amish women of the church from 7 a.m. to 9:30 a.m. There is also a lunch furnished by the Amish community and a bake sale. The auction is held on the farmstead of Rudy Beachy, 10433 Lindas Road, Readstown, WI 54652, phone 715-467-2800.

I want to thank the following people – listed in no particular order – for their support on this project. I couldn't have done it without you!

Arlene Morr, Karen Vonnen, Becky Wellington, Sherry Moore, Rose Westendorff, Mary Niswonger, Wilma Lentz, Jill Hershfield, June Hunte, Kimberly Hooper, John Chontofalsky, Aurora Toth, Sylvia Betz, Sondra Samples, Colleen Papp, Brenda Head, Karen Trible, Shane Bowlin, Bonnie Ornat, Dorrice Wallis, Chuck Hallam, Jerome Will, Mona Brewer, Carol Morris, Karen Parks, Mary Catherine Tyler, Vicki Van Wey, Anera Shell, Noreen Elliott, Margie Conrad, and James Zullig